SACRED
PASSAGE

SACRED PASSAGE

HOW TO PROVIDE
FEARLESS,
COMPASSIONATE
CARE FOR THE DYING

MARGARET COBERLY, Ph.D., R.N.

SHAMBHALA
Boston & London • 2002

Shambhala Publications, Inc.
Horticultural Hall
300 Massachusetts Avenue
Boston, Massachusetts 02115
www.shambhala.com

9 8 7 6 5 4 3 2

Printed in the United States of America

♾ This edition is printed on acid-free paper that meets the
American National Standards Institute Z39.48 Standard.
Distributed in the United States by Random House, Inc.,
and in Canada by Random House of Canada Ltd

Designed by Ruth Kolbert

Library of Congress Cataloging-in-Publication Data
Coberly, Margaret.
Sacred passage: how to provide fearless, compassionate care
for the dying/Margaret Coberly.—1st ed.
p. cm.
Includes bibliographical references and index.
ISBN 1-57062-850-5
1. Terminal care. 2. Compassion. 3. Death. I. Title
R726.8 C626 2002
616'.029—DC21
2001054182

To Venerable Karma Lekshe Tsomo

CONTENTS

ACKNOWLEDGMENTS

More than half of this book was written while traveling, and I am immensely grateful to the many people along the way who offered not only their gracious hospitality but also their strong emotional and financial support to facilitate my writing. First and foremost, I want to thank my mother, Elizabeth Stephens; my sister, Ceil Coberly; and my aunt, Margaret Coberly Hoover.

I also want to thank my mentor and friend psychology professor Samuel I. Shapiro for both his consistent, constructive, and good-humored counsel, and his unwavering insistence on meticulous scholarship. Without Sam's encouragement, I doubt that this book would have materialized.

The incredible generosity of many other people has contributed to the writing of this book. Jason Neal donated hours and hours of his precious time to edit the chapters as I wrote and rewrote them; and Asa Baber, Katherine Anderson, and my children, Ari and Ian, patiently listened to me and continually encouraged me no matter how boring it may have become for them. Ongoing conversations with Philippe Gross and Karma Lekshe Tsomo offered me reassurance and strength throughout the entire process, and the skill and uncanny insight of editor Eden Steinberg at Shambhala guided me to the finish. I am very grateful to each of them for their unique and wonderful help. I also want to acknowledge Miles Vich and Paul Clemens for their catalytic input at just the right moments.

The stories in this book are true, and I am forever indebted to all the patients and families who allowed me to be part of their dying trajectories. To protect their privacy, their names and other identifying characteristics have been changed, except in the case of my brother, Wheeler, and my cousin Cobe and his sons, Bud and Sterling.

I also want to thank and offer my deepest respect and admiration to the many wise and compassionate teachers of Tibetan Buddhism who have disseminated dharma teachings throughout the world and helped Western people become more aware of the Buddha's teachings. Most of the insights and theory that I am able to offer herein I have gleaned from reading or hearing the teachings of the fourteenth Dalai Lama, Kalu Rinpoche, Dilgo Khyentse, Lama ThubtenYeshe, Chagdud Tülku, Geshe Rabten, Gendün Chöpel, and the twelfth Tai Situ, as well as W. Y. Evans-Wentz, Herbert V. Guenther, Jeffrey Hopkins, and Robert A. F. Thurman.

My hope is that the information in this book will inspire its readers to overcome death denial and cultivate kindness and compassion towards people everywhere. May His Holiness the Dalai Lama and all other teachers of the truth live as long as possible, and may peace and happiness prevail on earth.

INTRODUCTION

*Any man's death diminishes me, because I am
involved in Mankinde; and therefore never
send to know for whom the bell tolls; it tolls
for thee.*

— JOHN DONNE, *Devotions*

When I was in nursing school a terminally ill child turned his big,
wondering eyes toward me and asked, "Am I going to die?" I was
stunned. What was I supposed to say? What *could* I say? I didn't
even know what I was allowed to say. Certainly I could not respond from my experience. Embarrassed and confused, I said
something like "Don't be silly! Of course you're not going to die.
You'll live to be a hundred," and then immediately changed the
subject. Wanting to feel safe, not threatened, I had retreated behind the mask of the mundane, and my heart closed. I did not feel
good about it, but back then I knew no other response. Like most
of my peers, I had reached adulthood without having talked much
about death. I was certainly not prepared to face it myself. In fact,
I had been deeply conditioned to believe that I was guaranteed a
bright future and a long life. Why would I think about death? No
one else did.

Nor was death a topic for study or reflection in my nurse's

training. This was unfortunate since, as a practicing nurse, I was surrounded by constant grief, pain, and death—often over-whelmed by it. I had few coping strategies. It was easy to adopt the customary aloofness of many health-care professionals, to distance myself from the anguish of my patients and their families. At times I heard about or was witness to certain events occurring around a death that seemed extraordinary and mysterious to me, but for the most part I viewed death the only way I knew how, with closed-minded indifference. By focusing on the disease, carrying out nursing functions dictated only by physical signs and symptoms, and relating to nurses and doctors rather than to patients, I was able to protect myself from thinking or feeling too much about death. Or so I thought. But my aloofness began to generate a new dissatisfaction—a disturbing feeling of being unkind. I felt a gnawing discomfort about my tendency to rush about busily preoccupied instead of giving a few moments of my time to genuinely comfort the bereaved. It was becoming evident that my unwillingness to face the fear of death had made me unavailable to human beings at a time when they most needed my genuine, compassionate presence.

I didn't fully realize just how unprepared I was to face death until my brother became terminally ill with a fast-growing lung cancer that was rapidly metastasizing, distributing malignancy throughout his body. For several weeks after his diagnosis I was unable to be of any real support or strength to him or anyone else, because I was so preoccupied with my own terror. I felt crippled just when my strength and comfort were needed the most. Death anxiety relentlessly pressed against my chest, and dread incapacitated me. The pressure soon became so unbearable that it forced me to turn inward and look at my own attitudes about death. To me death was a monstrous intrusion—an unwelcome, abnormal, and horrifying event. The prospect of death seemed chillingly final and unbelievably sad. I did not want to think about death, and I felt excruciatingly uncomfortable around dying people. But my brother needed me. And if I was to be a genuine presence during his dying trajectory, I would have to gain the knowledge required to overcome my fears. At this critical turning point I was forced to decide between making the effort to improve my understanding by facing death honestly, or doing nothing at all and returning to the comfort of my conditioned responses, denial and avoidance. I thought about how much easier it would be for me to bury myself in work, to pull double shifts in the emergency room and be simply too busy to face death with my brother. But one look into his terrified eyes and I knew I had no choice. Thus began my personal and professional research into thanatology—the study of death and the circumstances that surround a dying trajectory.

After my brother died, I practiced for several years as a hospice nurse and acquired much experience working with the terminally ill. At the same time, I began to work on a doctoral degree, studying psychology from both Western and Eastern perspectives. I began to relate certain behaviors I observed among my dying patients to what is described in psychology as the "transpersonal experience." For example, in working with dozens of dying people I observed that many of them would become deeply absorbed in a connection with some other source of power, of strength and understanding, that was beyond my comprehension as a professional caregiver. The meaning that I or any other caregiver might choose to assign to these observations was of little consequence to the dying person, who found great comfort in the experience.

I remember first hearing the word "transpersonal" and being baffled by it. I had no real idea what it meant. Through further investigation, I learned that definitions of such terms as *transpersonal psychology*, *transpersonal studies*, and *transpersonal experience* are still in the formative stages, but that, in general, the transpersonal approach embraces all of human experience and represents "action which takes place *through* a person, but which originates in a center of activity existing beyond the level of personhood,"[1] including the mysterious events that defy modern scientific explanation and transcend ordinary time and space concerns—for example, deathbed visions and near-death experiences, which have been reported by thousands of people. Even though scientific researchers have identified several patterns and themes in such reports, there is much about these events that remains beyond the reach of quantifiable measurement.

The Western medical paradigm, based on the scientific model of measurable "facts" and reproducible results, has enabled medicine to achieve astonishing feats over the last century. However, because of its single-minded focus on curing disease to the exclusion of all else, Western medicine has developed an unnecessarily limited view of health, illness, and dying. In particular, the Western medical paradigm has traditionally supported a theory that the mind and body have no connection, that the body is like a machine that when functioning improperly can be fixed by employing a strictly mechanical approach. Unfortunately, when a disease cannot be cured—when the machine cannot be fixed—the sick person is often deemed a medical failure, and, as a representative of defeat, he or she is often isolated, ignored, and avoided.

Over the past forty years, however, data from the emerging field of psychoneuroimmunology, which studies the connections between the mind and body down to the cellular level, has increasingly indicated that the mind does influence the condition of the body in extraordinary ways. For example, meditation has been shown to lower blood pressure,[2] and visualization has been shown to produce measurable changes in the immune system.[3] Knowledge about the mind's ability to affect the body has led to new views of illness and health—views in which patients are not seen as machines that are either broken or fixed. A broader definition of health and healing opens up the possibility that the dying, even with their unfixable and incurable diseases, have the potential for healing and the achievement of inner peace.

A primary step along the path toward healing in this deeper sense is to identify and reduce the stressful stimuli that prevent relaxation. A simple concentration technique for promoting relaxation has been developed by Western stress researchers,[4] and in Eastern cultures spiritual practices such as meditation and visualization have for centuries been known to reduce stress and promote inner balance and healing. It can be of great benefit to patients and their families if care providers have some knowledge about specific transpersonal techniques that can be used to assist in a healing process, particularly in the face of death.

Meditation, visualization, prayer, and self-reflection using such techniques as the life review[5] are practices that care providers can employ to assist a dying patient who wants to work toward growth and healing. Along with these approaches, I've found certain concepts and teachings from the Tibetan Buddhist tradition to be invaluable in my work with the dying.

I came to learn about Tibetan Buddhism purely by chance. One day, after my brother had been diagnosed with lung cancer, I went to the Bodhi Tree Bookstore in Los Angeles hoping to find solace in a book like *A Course in Miracles*. While browsing the shelves, I picked up a bright orange book that attracted me. It was *Advice from a Spiritual Friend* by Geshe Rabten and Geshe Dhargyey, and I wondered what "Geshe" meant (later I learned that it is an honored title given to those who complete an advanced academic degree in the Tibetan Buddhist monastic system). When I turned the book over to see the pictures of the authors, I was hooked from that moment. Their faces were full of so much peace and kindness—and there was no pretense. I started reading to find out how people get that way, how people actually achieve that kind of natural, relaxed happiness.

That was in 1987. About four years later when I was living in Hawaii, a friend encouraged me to attend a ceremony that was to be given by Tai Situ Rinpoche, a revered Tibetan teacher who was visiting Honolulu from India. I had been instructed that during the ceremony when I was standing before Rinpoche, I should lower my head and not look directly at him. But when I got right up next to him and bowed, I just couldn't stop myself. I looked up and met his eyes straight on, and all I can say is that it seemed like he zapped me somehow. It was very strange, but I suddenly felt deeply happy. Inspired by that experience, I continued to read about Tibetan Buddhism and dedicated myself to becoming a better person. In my reading I was pleased to discover many rich and detailed teachings on death—ideas that have given me great comfort and inspiration in my work with the dying.

According to Tibetan Buddhism, dying is not something to be feared, avoided, or denied, but rather something to be contemplated and appreciated as a special kind of opportunity. In this view, death can be an important teacher, allowing us to realize that impermanence underscores everything. All matter is subject to change; death is just the most profound reminder of that fact. My first conscious glimpses of the inescapable truth of death and the changing nature of all things were quite frightening because I was conditioned to deny these realities, not confront them. But slowly my acceptance of impermanence grew, and finally I was able to embrace the fact that everything changes. Although my hopes for achieving security in the external world were dashed, I gained an awareness of what Tibetan Buddhists call ceaseless transformation, a view of living and dying that I will present in this book in the hopes that it will be as helpful to other care providers as it has been to me.

Part One of the book explores the problem of death denial in Western health care. Here I'll share some striking stories that demonstrate how fear and denial harm the dying, their families, and health-care providers; and I'll explain why denial, fear, and avoidance of death have become so difficult to overcome. What's needed is a new understanding of death and a broader definition of healing, one that acknowledges the emotional and spiritual dimensions of health—dimensions that remain fertile even when people have a terminal disease. Part Two examines some of the central Tibetan Buddhist concepts and practices surrounding death. Although Tibetan Buddhism is not the only effective or important approach to confronting death honestly and openly, for me as a care provider, it has been a particularly valuable source of strength. The Tibetan tradition is replete with explicit, practical methodologies, and I found certain insights and applications that enabled me to start developing an attitude of receptivity toward the inevitability of change and death—a far cry from my earlier distancing strategy.

In Part Three I provide practical applications of the Tibetan teachings. These recommendations will be of use to anyone who must care for the dying, whether in a hospital, a hospice setting, or at home—or for anyone who has wondered what to say and how to behave around the dying.

My purpose in writing this book is to share with others the many lessons that I have learned both as a care provider to the dying and as a student of the Tibetan Buddhist teachings on death and dying. Feeling comfortable and present when facing a dying person requires more than knowledge learned in books; what is also needed is an inner humility and trust that comes from the actual experience of encountering death. The ability to provide healing care for the dying when cure is no longer a possibility involves cultivating skills that can be learned by most anyone who is willing to accept the task. Care providers and loved ones who further arm themselves with knowledge about alternative perspectives that broaden and strengthen their view of healing can greatly enrich their work with the dying. By becoming more receptive to the unusual events such as transpersonal experiences that often occur when a person is dying, care providers and loved ones alike are afforded an opportunity to find new meaning in the dying trajectory.

It has been an honor to be present during the final phase of life, and ultimate death, of many patients, friends, and relatives during my thirty -year career as a nurse. Every experience taught me more about the dying process, and about my own responses to it. The inner treasures of wisdom hidden in a dying trajectory are like jewels lying just beneath the surface. Facing death squarely not only eases a patient's passage out of this world; it can precipitate the emergence of some of these treasures, such as the deep recognition of the invariability of impermanence, or a clear awareness of the integrations that weave together everything in life and death. Care providers and patients alike have the ability to bring forth these and other treasures of the mind, when a resonant and healing spirit suffuses the dying trajectory.

PART ONE

DEATH
IN WESTERN
HEALTH CARE

O life as futile, then, as frail!
  O for thy voice to soothe and bless!
  What hope of answer, or redress?
Behind the veil, behind the veil.

ALFRED, LORD TENNYSON,
"In Memoriam"

I

The Problem
of Death Denial

> *Like one, that on a lonesome road*
> *Doth walk in fear and dread,*
> *And having once turned round walks on,*
> *And turns no more his head;*
> *Because he knows a frightful fiend*
> *Doth close behind him tread.*

> —SAMUEL TAYLOR COLERIDGE,
> "Rime of the Ancient Mariner"

DEATH IS DIFFICULT TO FACE. WE CAN'T control it, we barely understand it, and most of us are unwilling to talk about it. Ignoring the subject of death is widespread among us, and death denial our most common response. But death denial hurts us all. For if we are unable to find the courage to face death with openness, how are we to be truly compassionate with our loved ones when they are dying? Fear won't allow it. Although overcoming death denial is not easy, all of us who care for the dying—whether as family, friends, or health-care workers—must make an effort to face the task fearlessly, especially if we are to successfully meet the emotional and spiritual needs of those who depend on us for help when their lives are ending.

When my brother, Wheeler, died, some family members and friends denied that he was dying right up until the very end. Several friends stopped visiting altogether when his deteriorating physical condition challenged their denial. Wheeler would rest for hours gazing at some imaginary world of mystery. He would often reach out and pick at the air in front of him, and in broken whispers talk to people I couldn't see. "Lift me up, please lift me up," he'd often call out, as though sinking beneath a weight. People didn't know what to say when they saw him like that.

My father, in particular, had a very hard time facing Wheeler's impending death. He pretended that everything was the same as it had always been, and he refused to discuss that Wheeler was not getting well. Rather than sitting and talking with Wheeler, he spent his time investigating alternative chemical treatments and sending Wheeler's biopsy specimens to laboratories that offered experimental trial drugs.[1] He flew Wheeler to Canada one last time for some injections not yet approved in the United States, but nothing was able to impede the cancer's progression. My father personified security and permanence even when there was none, and he would not allow us to speak about the nearing of death even though its approach was glaringly obvious. One day he walked into Wheeler's room, his suit redolent with cigar smoke from his afternoon meeting at the California Club. Wheeler was lying in his shorts on the bed, with no bedcovers. His legs had dwindled to bones and his chest was completely sunken except for the grapefruit-sized tumor bulging out over his sternum and heart. Barely able to sip fluids, he was dry and withered. Dad looked at him and then glanced around apprehensively. I could see how uncomfortable he was. Death was a damnable and useless annoyance to him, definitely lacking elegance, intrigue, or profit. I knew that Wheeler felt ashamed for letting him down. To please Dad, he tried to lift his head up off the pillow and act like he was really okay. "I'm sorry, Dad," he said, "I guess I'm not doing very well." After a silence, a disturbing uneasiness, Dad said, "Oh, don't be ridiculous, you're going to be fine. Why don't I get you a vodka?" I felt so sad for all of us in that moment of pretense, yet because of my own fears and beliefs at the time I was unable to intercede with anything constructive or comforting.

Terminally ill patients themselves can be prone to death denial. I was the nurse for Martha, who had been diagnosed with ovarian cancer and whose prognosis was not good. She kept up a brave front for her friends, although her cancer had widely metastasized and was not responsive to chemotherapy. Her physician told her, "There is nothing more we can do to try and cure you, but we can offer you palliative care." When Martha became a hospice patient, she continued to deny her plight. Over and over she said, "I am going to beat this thing, if it is the last thing I do!" Her friends, too, were unwilling to face death and encouraged her to believe that she would "live to be a hundred." But as death inexorably continued to approach, Martha's deteriorating appearance betrayed all hope for recovery and her friends fell away in fright.

The anxiety that death engenders seems to discomfort some people so much that they withdraw completely and cannot tolerate being in the presence of a dying person, especially when it is a friend. Some confess that they simply do not know what to say. Yet even when assured that words are unnecessary, they find it impossible to face death. Fears about death and the dread of speaking about death separate people. During his terminal illness, sociologist Morrie Schwartz described the experience. He said that sick people are prone to feeling isolated and unhappy and loved ones to feeling guarded and afraid because everyone is trying to avoid talking about what is happening. "There is a kind of secrecy about illness," he wrote, "and it hurts us all."[2]

The harmful effects of death denial also became clear to me when my close friend Alexandra died. When she was released for the last time from Cedars-Sinai in Los Angeles, her physician finally informed her that there were no more curative treatments possible for her colon cancer and that palliative care was all he had left to offer. Alexandra wanted to stay out of the hospital at all costs and live at home for as long as she could. She never talked about her illness directly. It was almost as if she believed she would not die and that her disease was nothing more than a bad case of the flu that would eventually disappear. She asked me to come and live with her and her son while she tried to "get better." As the days passed her son and I watched her body waste away and her confusion grow. Often, she would float off into some world invisible to us and whisper strange words while she poked at the air in front of her. Her mother, who visited about twice a week, became more and more uncomfortable as Alexandra's attention increasingly drifted away from small talk and became immersed in conversation with someone no one else could see. "What's the matter with you?" her mother would demand sternly, "Who are you talking to? Stop it right now! I can't stand it!"

As Alexandra's condition worsened, most of her friends stopped coming by. It became too difficult for them to find something to say. The common clichés such as "You are doing great," "You have nothing to worry about," or "Chin up, you'll live to be a hundred" were particularly unfitting in this situation. Everyone sensed that she would not live, but most were unprepared to accept the fact that she was dying. On my first evening out in many weeks, I felt a tremendous sense of relief to get away from the pull of death for a while. I went to a dinner party where it was very comforting to be enveloped by the false impression of security evoked by so many well-dressed, nice-smelling people sitting at a huge mahogany table laden with rich food. In the middle of dinner I was pulled away to receive a panicky call from Alexandra's son. He asked in a voice filled with alarm, "Marg, what should we do? We thought Mom stopped breathing. She's breathing now, though, but 911 is coming, and we don't know what to do." The thought of Alexandra having to endure cardiopulmonary resuscitation made me shudder. I rushed home.

As I approached the driveway to her house, I saw an ambulance, a fire truck, and a police car parked outside the garage. Inside, emergency response personnel swarmed around Alexandra, who was lying on an ambulance stretcher, ready to be transported to the nearest emergency room. She looked frightened and confused. During her last round of chemotherapy all her hair had fallen out. Bald and jaundiced, she looked very near death. The rescue team was offended and angry that she wasn't in the hospital. One of the policemen took me aside and asked accusingly, "Does her doctor know about her condition? Doesn't she belong in the hospital where they can take care of her? She looks like . . . she looks like she's . . ." He couldn't find the words. "Like she's dying," I said. "She *is* dying, and she wants to die here in her own familiar environment, not in an indifferent hospital." I was beginning to feel like a criminal and that maybe we really were doing something wrong.

When the response team finally left, they were shaking their heads in disbelief that neither Alexandra nor I wanted her to be rushed to the hospital. In their minds Alexandra would somehow be saved from death if only she would go to the safety of the hospital. It was a troubling event. It made me start to have some reservations. I began to question whether we were pursuing the right course of action by keeping her at home. Maybe it *would* be better for her to be in the hospital, I thought. I called her doctor to talk it over, and he said, "Well, okay, sure, we can put her back in, but you know that goes against her wishes. We could pump her up with some fluids overnight—that is if we are able to establish a line in her vein; otherwise I would have to insert a central-venous catheter to deliver the fluids, and she hates that." After further discussion we decided together to honor Alexandra's wishes, and she died at home several days later. I remained amazed at the sheer force and pervasive power of conventional death denial and how easily I had succumbed to it with my own doubts. Such denial has strongly persisted in the United States for most of the twentieth century, abetted by the powerful influence of the Western medical paradigm, with its focus on aggressive treatment and cure: it is a model that characterizes death as a failure.

The Prevailing Medical Paradigm

In the West, treatment and cure have been the main objectives of medical care, leaving the psychological aspects of dying for the patient to cope with alone.[3] The Western model concentrates on aggressive treatment designed to reverse a disease process. This curing model of care, preoccupied with the diagnosis and treatment of physical signs and symptoms, tends to ignore the emotional needs and existential questions that most patients also have.

With its heavy emphasis on technology and cure, the prevailing Western medical paradigm is a fitting backdrop for our national preoccupation with speed, youth, beauty, and endurance— obsessions that have driven medicine to innovative and successful heights in its ability to cure disease, prolong life, retard aging, and even restore youthful appearance. Hundreds of surgical procedures are available to enliven failing hearts, replace worn-out organs, realign facial features, reduce fat, remove wrinkles, and replenish collagen. Spectacular lifesaving techniques have been developed to actually rescue a person who has clinically died.

Forty years ago, if a person stopped breathing for more than a few minutes, oxygen deprivation would cause the heart to fail and the brain to stop functioning, and the patient would die.[4] Since then, the use of external cardiac shock, cardiopulmonary and mouth-to-mouth resuscitation, mechanical ventilators, and powerful new drugs have changed the course of the "normal" dying process forever. People now live longer. Technological advances have yielded unprecedented opportunities not only for extending a healthy life, but also for prolonging an unhealthy one. Longer life spans, lingering deaths, and ever-improving life support systems contribute to a recent estimate that in the United States one in eight Americans is over the age of sixty-five, and that by 2020 it will be one in five.[5] We increasingly need health-care providers who have conquered their own denial and fear of death, and who have cultivated knowledge and expertise about what happens during a dying trajectory.

The palliative model of care concentrates on meeting a patient's emotional, mental, and spiritual needs, while at the same time treating the physical signs and symptoms produced by the disease. Healing—the restoration of a person's sense of inner balance and harmony—is at the heart of palliative care and can be achieved even if a cure cannot. Because the population of elderly people who are dying is increasing so rapidly, it has become critically important for care providers to be comfortable when interacting with dying patients. Unfortunately, many physicians and nurses—viewed as the most reliable sources of information and guidance during illness—express strong feelings of incompetence when it comes to interacting with the dying.[6] Studies have shown that nurses and physicians report anxiety and a sense of incompetence because they are not academically prepared to cope with the stresses of working with dying patients and patients' families.[7]

Nurses, the professional care providers who traditionally spend the most time with dying patients and their families, have been shown in some studies to spend as much as 50 percent of the time they communicate with terminal patients employing avoidance behaviors such as changing the subject of conversation or giving premature advice or reassurance.[8] It's news that would make Florence Nightingale, the founder of professional nursing, turn over in her grave. Referring to such avoidance behavior in her journal entry entitled "chattering hopes the bane of the sick," she wrote:

> There is no one practice against which I can speak more strongly. I would appeal most seriously to all . . . attendants of

the sick to leave off this practice of attempting to "cheer" the sick by making light of their danger and by exaggerating their probabilities of recovery. . . . The patient . . . feels isolated in the midst of friends. He feels what a convenience it would be, if there were any single person to whom he could speak simply and openly, without pulling the string upon himself of this shower-bath of silly hopes and encouragements.[9]

There are several reasons why a health-care professional might feel unprepared to face the dying. Physicians, for example, undergo long, rigorous training on how to keep ailing people alive, regardless of any other circumstances, and as a result, most of them tend to view the death of a patient as a failure on their part. Such a view causes many of them to avoid interaction with a patient who is dying. The Hippocratic Oath, written more than two thousand years ago, continues to guide physicians today. By taking the oath, a physician vows to maintain life above all else—a mandate that is adhered to even when a patient is extremely old, worn out, and actively striving to die naturally and peacefully. As a result the myth that aggressive treatment is the only proper and ethical course of action, even for the incurable, is perpetuated within the health-care profession. Most physicians are completely focused on problem solving and can afford little time interacting with the dying.

Physician Elisabeth Kübler-Ross remarked about her medical training, "There is nothing in the system that provides for human nurturance to the soul when the body is beyond repair."[10] The meaning of her words became graphically clear to me one afternoon while I was working in the trauma room of a large hospital. The paramedics wheeled in a ninety-five-year-old woman who had been receiving chemotherapy and radiation for a metastasized cancer that was growing throughout her emaciated body. Sallow skin hung from her arms and legs, and she looked dehydrated and parched. Her top lip was retracted, exposing her yellow, caked teeth. Her eyes were glazed and fixed, and rolled upward. Her body was used up. She had died, but resuscitation was in full swing. I could hear her ribs snapping like dry sticks beneath the cardiac compressions. She was revived: Another jubilant victory for medicine. The patient, however, lay alone, confused, wild-eyed, and in agony, and then died again amidst a jumble of tubes, needles, masks, and distracted personnel.

Nursing School and Death Denial

In nursing school I believed that the hospital was the safest place anyone could possibly be: people came in with a problem and left without it. Fixing seemed guaranteed. My belief at the time was that physicians were beyond error. The uniform of anonymity that I wore was the same for all the students: a white starched pinafore over a blue pinstripe dress. The pinafore rustled loudly, making the sound of approaching students a familiar one, impossible to disguise. When I started my rotation in cancer nursing, I had been prepared for the experience by attending classes that focused on facts regarding the physical effects of aggressive treatments such as chemotherapy, radiation, and surgery, and ways to make a patient who was undergoing such treatment more comfortable. There was no mention of death.

My first patient on the cancer ward was a young girl of fifteen, Sandra, who was being treated with chemotherapy for a fast-growing cancer. She looked extremely ill, but I thought it was the result of side effects from the experimental chemotherapy she was receiving. I believed that she would eventually recover and go home. I certainly did not consider the possibility that she might die. Nevertheless, one day, when I walked into her room, she was lying there, dead. The head nurse was standing near the bed and was surrounded by several distraught family members. I looked at Sandra's face. It was frozen in an expression of agony and her jaw hung loosely, exposing her teeth.

At this point the doctor came swooping into the room and

approached the bedside to formally pronounce Sandra dead. He hastily addressed the grieving family, telling them they could call his office for any information they might need, but adding that he was late for a meeting. He turned and quickly left, the head nurse trailing after him. Completely bewildered that he'd abandoned us all so abruptly, I stood there dumbfounded as the family turned to me for support. Death had never been discussed in any of my classes. I did not know what to do or say. I felt very incompetent and confused, and started to cry along with everyone else. The next day in class, I asked the instructor what a nurse was supposed to do in the event of a death. She replied, "You cover the face with a sheet, and straighten the linen on the bed, so that it looks nice for the family. You must try to cheer them up." That was the end of the discussion and my formal education on dealing with a death scene.

After completing the cancer rotation in nursing school, I was assigned to the burn unit—an area where many gravely ill patients hung in a delicate balance between life and death. There was a huge tub in the middle of the room, and almost always there was a severely burned patient soaking or being cleaned in it. A radio played softly to calm restless nerves. One day, the radio music abruptly stopped and an agitated and emotional announcement was broadcast: "President Kennedy has been shot. While riding through the crowds shortly after his arrival in Dallas, Texas, today, the President was hit by an assassin's bullet."

All of us—patients and care providers alike—shared in the shocking and horrifying realization that the President had been shot. Each of us clung to the belief that he was only wounded, until we heard the next pronouncement: "The President of the United States is dead." It was an eerie and charged moment—everything stood still—as each person in the room tried to grasp the meaning of what had happened. There was an overwhelming need to deny the event. "It just can't be true" was the sentiment heard everywhere. The gripping incident brought the subject of death out of the closet for a while. Soon, though, veils of distraction reemerged and people were lulled back into the safety net of denial.

Although the subject of death would occasionally arise in nursing school as a startled response to some dramatic event such as Kennedy's death, it was not regarded as an important ongoing topic. Most other death education that occurred at the time focused on medical or legal matters such as the prevention or cause of a death, but the subject of death itself was ignored. I remember one afternoon when a forty-year-old woman was admitted to the ward where I was assigned. She had come to San Francisco with her husband and daughter to sightsee and shop. Suddenly, though, she had developed a high fever of unknown origin and was rushed to the hospital for treatment. Another student and I helped admit the woman to room 315. I took her temperature: it was 104 degrees, somewhat lower than it had been one hour before in the emergency room downstairs. We undressed her quickly, helped her into bed, and gave her a cooling alcohol sponge bath. The physician ordered intravenous fluids and said that he would start antibiotics as soon as he learned the results of the blood tests that had been done earlier in the emergency room. I was at the nurses' station writing my student report about the experience when I heard "Code blue 315, code blue 315" called out over the loud speaker. "Code blue" meant that a patient had suffered cardiac arrest and needed immediate help from the hospital's emergency cardiac team. I jumped up and ran to room 315. There were many people crowding around the bed, attaching pads for the electrocardiograph machine and inserting needles and catheters. I could barely see what was happening. I could tell that the woman was sitting upright against the back of the bed just as we had left her, but when the physician pushed a back board behind her so that he could start chest compressions, she fell forward, limp and expressionless, against his shoulder.

My instructor came to the door and pulled me away. With tears in her eyes, she said, "Go back to the classroom now, we can talk about this later." I saw the woman's husband and daughter walking toward the room as I was leaving the ward. I glanced at them quickly, then averted my eyes. Although I felt a rush of sympathy for them, I was very glad to be leaving the scene altogether. I was filled with terror about the swiftness of the woman's death. It didn't seem possible that a person could be swallowed up by death so fast. It made no sense at all to me and I was dazed. To look any of the family members in the eye, or attempt to talk with them, was something I was unprepared to do. Later, the instructor and I cried together and she talked about the seriousness of fevers, especially those that have no known origin, but she said nothing about the death, or the feelings of the family members who had been left to grieve alone. Even though it was vitally important for us as student nurses to learn how to adequately cope with death and dying, most of us left nursing school with little or no education about it.

As a young nurse, I was particularly embarrassed and confused around the dying. In the face of death my rote habitual responses seemed inept. I felt awkward and busied myself with chores, tiptoeing around pretending that the patient was asleep. The prospect of being in the presence of a dying person combined with my ignorance about dealing with the situation disturbed me. When I was talking with a dying patient, I babbled on mindlessly, hoping to avoid drifting into unfamiliar territory. I protected myself with action and speed—being busy—and so went into emergency nursing, where events are continually unfolding and changing quickly. Deaths in the emergency room happened very fast. Any single death became a blur of lost memory in the stream of circumstances that were constantly evolving there. There was no time or need to reflect on death: it was sad, yes, but why dwell on it?

Emergency Room Practice

In the late 1970s, when I was working in an emergency department in Spanish Harlem in New York City, it was known that

I had recently participated in an at-home hospice program, and as a result, when there was a death in the department I would be sought out to "break the news" to the loved ones. Most of the physicians, only able to shudder at a death, tended to scurry away after pronouncing a patient dead. "I'll buy you lunch if you talk to the family," was an offer I commonly received. Even some of the nurses came to rely on me as the bearer of sad news; none of us really felt competent to deal with it.

I was usually frightened as I approached the family members who had been waiting for hours for information about a loved one's condition. Their heads would turn with anticipation every time the emergency room door swung open. Telling people that a loved one has died is an extremely delicate task. Each person involved has a different relationship to the deceased; each feels his or her own situation the most acutely. Together, the family and I would walk to a more private area—an uninviting room containing metal chairs etched with graffiti and wastepaper baskets brimming over with fast-food containers. After everyone was seated and silent for a moment, an unusual tension would fill the room as the group began to feel the nearness of death. Then I would softly deliver my lines: "Everything possible was done. The doctors, the nurses, everyone involved, worked hard to prevent this outcome, but I am so sorry to tell you that your brother (or mother, father, sister, grandmother, son, lover, cousin, daughter, wife, baby) has died." A moment of heavy silence usually followed, laden with unexpressed implications as each individual struggled with his or her own reactions to the finality of death, closely followed by sobs. Then denial: "No, no, it just can't be, I don't believe it!"

I would sit quietly with the survivors and listen to the stories about their relationships with the deceased. Sometimes I would cry with them. Occasionally people would respond in unpredictable ways to news about the death of a loved one. One time, a man suddenly grabbed a lamp from the table and threw it at me, yelling, "All you damn doctors don't know nothin' about nothin'!"

Another time a woman tore the sleeve off my scrub dress as she screamed with condemnation, "You killed my husband, you killed him, you bitch!" Two Puerto Rican women responded to the news of their brother's fatal overdose by throwing themselves onto the floor and rolling frantically from side to side. Nothing I had learned in nursing school or anywhere else had geared me for the situations I was now experiencing as a practicing nurse. But I was beginning to see the way that death denial had crept into almost every corner of daily life and rendered us all less able to face the reality of our own mortality.

Death Denial in the Community

Death denial is evident in community life throughout the United States, especially in places like nursing homes, where large numbers of the elderly and infirm live out the end of their lives.[11] I went to have lunch one day with a friend who was the medical director of a nursing home. He took me on a tour through the various patient areas and introduced me to several people, and then led me into a large room where ten patients lay in beds that were lined up against the far wall. I went from bedside to bedside looking at each of the patients. Most of them appeared to be almost dead. The ones who didn't have a feeding tube protruding from their nose had an intravenous line dripping fluids into one of their veins. All appeared to be completely oblivious to their surroundings, and none seemed aware of our presence in the room. These patients were being kept alive artificially even after any prospect of a useful or satisfying life had passed, simply because death was not acceptable to their next of kin. Perhaps a few of them, at an earlier time, had told loved ones that they wanted to cling to life at all costs, but more likely most of them had failed to make their wishes known to anyone at all. And in such cases, care providers are legally required to do everything possible to prolong life.[12]

Later, when lunch was served, I observed a number of the very old and debilitated people there being spoon-fed against their will. One nurse was manually opening her patient's jaw and forcing food into his mouth, saying, "You don't want to have a feeding tube, now do you?" Death denial in care providers causes them to be unreceptive to the fact that people eventually do die, regardless of everyone's best attempts to prevent it from happening. Death denial also blocks our ability to understand that some very elderly people who have no hope for recovery may no longer experience meaning in life and may want to die naturally by stopping their food intake. Worried care providers usually respond by forcing the person to eat or inserting a feeding tube, regardless of the patient's wishes.

Most people are so strongly habituated to death denial that when death appears they are caught entirely by surprise. Overwhelmed and confused, they tend to miss out on the extraordinary opportunity for peace and resolution that is inherent in the dying trajectory. Death denial permeates people's lives in many different ways and powerfully influences the choices they make. Theresa, for example, was a middle-aged woman diagnosed with liver cancer. During Theresa's last office visit, her physician told her that the chemotherapy treatments she had been receiving were no longer working. "For the past several months," the physician explained, "the treatment has had no effect other than to dangerously lower your blood cell counts and reduce your resistance to infection. So, I am tripling your pain medication and want you to come back and see me in two weeks." Theresa wasn't informed about the gravity of her untreatable liver cancer, nor was she given any explanation about her prognosis or what she might expect in the following weeks.

Theresa and her husband clung to the comforting adage "No news is good news," and did not press for answers to their lingering doubts. Thus, even though Theresa was extremely unwell, she and her husband arrived home with their hopes bolstered by death denial. They reasoned that Theresa would be all right because "the doctor didn't mentioned anything about hospice, besides, a person has to have a terminal diagnosis to get into hospice."[13] Under the spell of denial, Theresa explained away her illness as a condition from which she would soon recover. She forced herself to sit at the dinner table and to carry on other activities as if all that was required for a cure was just a little more time. As the days passed, her eyes darkened with jaundice, her gait faltered, and her mind increasingly clouded. The physical deterioration was difficult to mistake. One morning, despite her best efforts to appear normal, her eyes began to uncontrollably roll back into her head and she seemed to be drifting in and out of a comalike state. Deeply alarmed, her husband telephoned the physician, who immediately referred Theresa to the local hospice. She died that night, just eight days after her last visit to the physician.

Theresa and her family had wanted to fill their lives with hope, and quite naturally leaned toward avoiding thoughts about the possibility of death—an attitude supported, even shared, by the health professionals who had guided them. But such an approach not only deprived Theresa of the opportunity to prepare for her impending death; it also robbed her and her family of the chance to resolve old problems and say good-bye.

Death denial deceives us into believing that death will not come. Yet death does come, regardless of our great desire for it not to be so. And when it does arrive, the sadness and sense of loss that occurs is intensified beyond measure when we are unprepared. Life craves life, and curative care is the most common and instinctive choice any of us make when our life is threatened by disease. It is natural to want to do everything possible to prevent or forestall death. Yet there are times when choosing curative care may in itself bring immense and debilitating problems that interfere with the chance to heal during the last phase of life. Lyle's case is an example.

Lyle was diagnosed with a type of cancer that could be treated with a series of painful, nauseating chemotherapy infusions and injections that would be given intermittently over a two-year period. The physician briefly mentioned that the treatment, although quite efficient in effecting a cure in some patients, was also capable of causing another kind of cancer to develop in others. She quickly recited statistics that were not very encouraging; for example, she said that only about 20 percent of the patients who underwent such treatment had survived for more than two years after it ended. But without the stomach-turning chemotherapy, Lyle's life expectancy was projected to be less than one year. Thus, regardless of the slim chance for survival it offered, and the future illnesses it was known to produce, the chemotherapy treatment was both the physician's and Lyle's immediate choice, just as it would have been for most people.

For the next year and a half Lyle endured a punishing series of infusions and injections that were consistently effective, first at reducing the size of the cancer tumor and then later at eradicating it altogether. Everyone rejoiced. Lyle was "beating the cancer," and his physicians applauded their medical victory. Soon, though, a new and very different kind of highly virulent cancer rapidly developed in Lyle's blood cells and he abruptly died. In this poignant situation, Lyle's care providers, in their rush to eliminate Lyle's primary cancer, had forged ahead with the toxic treatment without adequately emphasizing to Lyle and his family that there was a strong possibility of serious negative consequences occurring along with the hoped-for positive ones. Had both the pros and the cons of treatment been more fully discussed, Lyle and his family might have been better prepared for the outcome. Instead, almost everyone involved in Lyle's dying process wholeheartedly supported a stance of denial, entertaining and encouraging false hopes throughout the treatment because they created a solid barrier against having to discuss the unwelcome possibility of death. Lyle and his caregivers resisted the likelihood of death, and as a result he lost the chance to fully and openly experience the final stage of his life.

During a dying trajectory, there are many emotional hurdles to overcome and physical problems to solve. The days pass quickly and death advances relentlessly. This is a period of tenuous waiting and delicate timing that, when not impeded by death denial, can be an opportunity for new possibilities to open and for wisdom to deepen. Most of us strive for meaning in our lives and in our relationships, and the nearing of death brings urgency to that effort. For this reason alone, it is imperative that the prevailing medical model be revised to include a more expansive and holistic view of healing.

2

A Broader View
of Healing

Near or far,
Hiddenly
To each other linkèd are,
That thou canst not stir a flower
Without troubling of a star . . .

— FRANCIS THOMPSON,
"The Mistress of Vision"

HEALING CAN OCCUR FOR A PATIENT EVEN when there is no hope for a cure. Healing in this sense embraces a broader perspective than curing, and includes the complex and interdependently woven scheme of emotional, mental, and spiritual energies that define the individual beyond his or her biological history. In the healing process, an understanding about the deeper needs a patient might express is just as important as knowing the cause of the physical disease and how to alleviate its symptoms. Healing requires open-mindedness about all the events that occur during a dying trajectory, even the extraordinary and mysterious ones that are usually overlooked in the strictly curative model of care.

A healing model of care works toward the restoration of a person's sense of equilibrium and harmony, even when the body is in a state of decline and demise. Dying people who are given the opportunity to heal are often able to resolve difficult relationships, develop new understandings about themselves, and enrich their own and others' lives with the acceptance of death. Healing is important for people who are dying because it ultimately leads to the discovery of inner peace—a state that can bring immense satisfaction and comfort at the end of life. People who are dying may go through many different stages of self-discovery as they heal. Unfortunately, their journey can be inhibited or even cut short by well-meaning loved ones and care providers who themselves are in denial and therefore feel awkward and uncomfortable about discussing and contemplating death with the dying person.

There is a great need in the United States for more dialogue about death and dying, and for more information about alternative medical perspectives that are focused on healing and palliative care. Yet discussions about death and dying are commonly avoided, and treatment modalities outside the traditional biomedical model are generally shunned. Fortunately, over the last forty years a healing model of palliative care for the terminally ill has slowly become a more accepted part of the health-care system in America. This is due in large part to the pioneering efforts of one physician, Elisabeth Kübler-Ross.

Kübler-Ross and the Plight of the Dying

The plight of the dying and their need for healing were topics almost completely ignored in the United States prior to the research and writings of Elisabeth Kübler-Ross—the first physician in America to bring the taboo subject of death out of the closet and into public awareness. Kübler-Ross repeatedly observed that for nurses and doctors alike it was often easier and less threatening to avoid any psychological interaction around the dying than it was to risk getting involved in a discussion about something as terrifying as death. She focused public awareness on how the needs of the dying were not being met because of the unpopularity of death as a subject for dialogue and reflection.

Kübler-Ross recognized that dying involves not only the final deterioration of a body but also the passing of an individual. She began to talk openly to dying patients about the isolation and desperation that so many of them experienced. Her observations led her to hypothesize that from the time people first receive a terminal diagnosis until the time they die, most experience one or more of a series of five distinct psychological stages: denial, anger, bargaining, depression, and acceptance.[1] Kübler-Ross viewed these psychological stages as dynamic and fluid, not sequential, and she proposed that people pass through them according to their own individual psychological needs. Later, Kübler-Ross went on to develop her theory even further by suggesting that there were two additional stages after the first five: a stage of life review and completion of old business, and a stage of transcendence where the dying person's awareness expands to include a more universal, or transpersonal,[2] dimension of reality that lies beyond the constraints of individual limitations and the boundaries of space and time.

One important method that Kübler-Ross used to teach care providers about death was to have certain dying patients meet with and talk to her medical students and colleagues. In these meetings, the dying patients would describe in detail what they were personally experiencing physically and emotionally. Some would also offer suggestions about what they thought physicians could do to improve care of the dying in general. Even though decades have passed since Kübler-Ross first began her groundbreaking research into the needs of the dying, palliative care for the terminally ill continues to be a concept that is not entirely understood or accepted, especially by the many practitioners who adhere strictly to the Western medical model.

The former president of the American Academy of Hospice and Palliative Medicine reports that palliative medicine is widely acknowledged throughout England and Australia, where it has been established as a medical specialty; however, in the United States it has yet to reach formal recognition.[3] Palliative care for the dying is extremely important because its focus on healing can help people achieve understanding, resolution, and peace at the end of life.

Palliative Care and Healing

My personal experience with a palliative model of care—or hospice—began in New York City during the 1970s. At that time the concept was very new in the United States, and it was difficult, almost impossible, to adequately manage the symptoms of a terminally ill patient who was not in a hospital.[4] But when a friend of mine, Allison, became terminally ill, she asked to be cared for in her apartment, not in a hospital. Allison and I, as children, had lived on the same block in Los Angeles and had ridden our tricycles down the same sidewalks. Later, as debutantes, we had danced and partied together in long white dresses and vied for the same handsome beaus, but it wasn't until she became very sick that I really got to know her.

Allison had been given a prognosis of three months to live by her oncologist at the Memorial Sloan-Kettering Cancer Institute. How or where she was supposed to do the dying was not discussed, but for her, dying in the hospital was not an option. Several of us decided to take the responsibility for setting up an at-home dying situation for Allison, and we formed a team. Three nurses, two doctors, and about fifteen friends worked out the details for her physical care and overall well-being. We experienced firsthand the difference between learning about death and dying from books, and the actual experience of a dying trajectory. Many of the solutions to the dilemmas we encountered in Allison's care had to be improvised as each new situation unfolded.

A tranquil and peaceful environment was created in Allison's apartment so that she could visit with her children and friends and continue with her meditation practice. Weekly meetings kept the team coordinated and running smoothly. The biggest problem became Allison's increasing level of pain, and the oncologist's decreasing willingness to prescribe an adequate amount of pain medication. We had heard about Brompton's solution, a mixture providing excellent pain relief for cancer patients in England. However, Brompton's contained ingredients, such as heroin, that are illegal for this kind of use in the United States. In fact, physicians traditionally treated the pain associated with terminal cancer in the same way that they treated any other kind of pain—on a prescribed schedule and from an addiction-prohibitive point of view.

There were no established hospices in New York City then, and a general lack of understanding prevailed about the needs of the dying, and the importance of palliative care.[5] Allison's team had to find alternative methods, outside her primary physician's care plan, to meet her needs and to control her excruciating pain. One of the physicians on the team calculated a very effective mixture of different drugs that when given together seemed to strengthen the pain control: an injection of morphine, a rectal suppository of Compazine, one-half teaspoon of cocaine dissolved in a tablespoon of cognac sweetened with honey. Later, when the oncologist learned that it was costing more than three hundred dollars a week for the team to buy illegal "street" cocaine to use as a potentiator for Allison's morphine injections, he finally relented and prescribed pharmaceutical cocaine. After Allison died, we all felt that our efforts to achieve a healing environment for her—one that tried to meet her physical, mental, emotional, and spiritual needs—had been successful.

Interestingly enough, the difficulty we experienced twenty years ago in obtaining sufficient pain control continues to be a problem for some patients and their physicians today, except within health-care environments that focus on palliative or hospice care.[6] Even there, some hospice nurses report that much of their job stress continues to be related to a general lack of open communication and support from physicians who do not understand the principles of palliative care. Aside from ignorance or misinformation about pain control, other popular misconceptions about death and dying hinder adequate palliative care—for example, the widely held beliefs that preparation for death is morbid, that reconciliation with death isn't possible, and that people who are dying don't really want to know that they are dying. These misunderstandings are formed within the framework of death denial and are responsible for much of the isolation and abandonment that many dying people in the United States continue to express today.

Palliative care not only encourages preparation for death but also offers the dying person an opportunity to reconcile with life by facing death. For example, physician Ira Byock, author of *Dying Well*, uses a process of life review that often helps his dying patients gain a sense of meaning about their life and opens them to the transcendent dimension that lies beyond the boundaries and limits of the individual self. Other unconventional approaches that are used in palliative care, such as prayer, meditation, visualization, and music therapy, also draw on a source of wisdom that lies within the person, but is transpersonal and extends beyond the person, the illness, and the sense of individual separation.

The palliative model of care openly acknowledges the fact that some human experience may involve phenomena beyond the existing scope of science and medicine.[7] From this perspective, nonordinary states are not considered pathological or frightening, but are seen as potent catalyzers that can unlock the human potential for growth, transformation, and healing.

Healing and the Power of the Mind

Mind-body studies have shown that a person's physical condition can be measurably changed by his or her state of mind. Chronic stress, for example, has been shown to have many deleterious effects on the body. It is well known that people who live in a constant state of stress are more prone to heart disease and other debilitating conditions. Stress researcher Herbert Benson developed an antidote for stress he called the "relaxation response."[8] He demonstrated how a simple two-step technique— (1) repetition of a word, sound, prayer, or phrase, and (2) a reflexive return to the repetition whenever everyday thoughts intrude—can decrease a person's metabolism, heart rate, blood pressure, rate of breathing, and even the amplitude of the brain's alpha waves.[9] Benson says the technique is universally successful in reducing stress because "it is like penicillin—it will work whether or not you believe in it."[10]

Mental conditions other than stress, such as those generated by strong emotions like fear, sorrow, hatred, joy, humor, and love, have also been shown to cause specific biochemical brain changes that trigger a cascade of events in the body that affect health.[11] Other studies have shown that negative emotions can reduce the ability of the immune system to protect against invading microbes and that positive emotions can enhance systems that lead to better pain tolerance or increased healing.[12] Emotions have also been shown to produce measurable biochemical changes that can be detected throughout the entire body, not just in the brain—a finding that suggests every cell has intelligence and that the mind is present throughout the whole body.[13] What a person believes and expects can significantly influence and even condition the immune system. In addition to being able to induce measurable physiological responses, beliefs and expectations have been shown to influence other outcomes.[14] Studies about self-fulfilling prophecy, for example, have established that a person or group's expectation of a certain outcome produces behaviors that greatly increase the likelihood of that outcome occurring.[15]

Although current mind-body research reveals that thoughts, beliefs, and emotions play a significant role in determining the quality of both physiological and psychological events in an individual, most people are unaware of the extraordinary ability they have to influence their own well-being. Even for people who have experienced the great inner happiness that can result from fostering positive beliefs and spontaneous emotions, it is often easier to react with negative, conditioned habits based on the past. One negative habit that most of us have in common is to worry, especially in stressful situations. Rather than responding to events spontaneously and creatively, the worried person imagines all the possible terrible outcomes that could happen. Even if the negative fantasies never actually materialize, just thinking about them can produce deleterious biochemical changes in the physiology of the body.

Seventy-five years ago in medicine the physiological effects produced by nonspecific factors such as negative or positive thoughts and feelings were referred to as the "placebo effect." At one time, physicians greatly valued the power of the placebo effect. Some suggested that physicians themselves ought to be able to elicit a positive placebo response just through a consultation with a patient.[16] As more specific and powerful treatments such as antibiotics, insulin, and open-heart surgery were developed, the medical community came to rely on them exclusively and the nonspecific influences were forgotten. However, the power of the mind to affect the body and transform and heal the whole person is a concept slowly becoming popular again as mind-body research reveals through scientific measurement the exquisitely interwoven nature of the mind and the body.

During World War II, Victor Frankl, a physician imprisoned in the Nazi concentration camps, wrote compellingly about the strength of mind he observed in certain prisoners—men who were able to sustain a satisfactory life and to hope for future happiness, even while surrounded by the brutal hatred and dehumanized living conditions that existed in the camps. Frankl noted that these prisoners were identified with and found meaning in something greater than the individual self. By expanding their existential awareness, they were fortified by an energy and power that seemed to lie outside the boundaries of conventional thinking, beyond the everyday vicissitudes of life. Frankl wrote: "Man can, through loving contemplation of the image he carries . . . achieve fulfillment. . . . For the first time in my life I was able to understand the meaning of the words, 'The angels are lost in perpetual contemplation of an infinite glory.' "[17] Somehow, seeing a vision in the mind and reinforcing it with repetition brings it to life.

Investigation into the effects of visualization on people, illness, and healing began in the scientific community after a remarkable discovery was made: Many people who experience a spontaneous remission of their disease also constantly hold a vision of themselves as well again.[18] Further study made it clear that visualization can produce beneficial changes in an individual that are measurable both physiologically and psychologically. Visualization is used in various ways by modern medicine today. Some practitioners have incorporated it in the form of guided imagery to effectively help cancer patients overcome the nausea associated with chemotherapy and the fear that accompanies impending surgery.[19] Visualization can also be used to help people overcome the negative concepts inherent in death denial. When stereotypical beliefs about death that generate fear and confusion are replaced with positive images that bring peace of mind, a person can begin to overcome death denial. Instead of denying the possibility of death, a person with an incurable disease can visualize a healing process that has a positive and fulfilling outcome in terms of personal growth and transcendent understanding.

Prayer is another way to concentrate the mind on positive outcomes, and people throughout history have relied on it as a way to transcend suffering and promote healing. More than one hundred years ago, Francis Galton, a researcher known for his extraordinary scientific rigor, studied the effects of prayer on illness. Galton was unable to find a measurable effect, yet he advocated prayer for the positive influence it had on people's attitude toward illness and healing.[20] Today, researchers have demonstrated that prayer can have a measurably beneficial effect on healing.[21] During the dying process, for example, the consoling power of prayer can open people to the transcendent realm and nurture healing by cultivating compassion, caring, empathy, and love. Prayer reaches beyond the ordinary world to a realm that lies beyond the physical body and physical death.

As denial becomes an increasingly ineffectual way to cope with death, the genuine need for a revisioning of old negative reactions to death and dying grows. The negative death beliefs that are developed within a framework of denial slowly begin to dissolve when positive beliefs are cultivated instead. To hold positive beliefs—to hope—opens individuals to new possibilities. When a person lets go of preconceived ideas about death and moves beyond denial, the transformative potential of the human mind becomes apparent. Once people become aware of the power they have to determine their own happiness simply by altering the way they perceive their circumstances—even the circumstance of imminent death—they can begin to heal.

Reflecting on Death

Since the quality of life for a dying person can be positively influenced by open and honest interactions, it is imperative that all of us—professional and lay people alike—begin to dismantle the conspiracy of silence that has enshrouded death for so long, and work to transform our fear and denial into knowledge and acceptance. One powerful way to begin understanding death is to consciously reflect on it. Just sit quietly and think about death for a minute. It's not easy! Having denied it for so long, we can't help but find it difficult to imagine death at all. What does death look like? One important and obvious realization that can come to light when thinking about death is that death is inevitable. The time death will come is uncertain, but that it will arrive is irrefutable. Everything and everyone now alive will one day be dead. This recognition—that death cannot be overcome—strikes a fatal blow to the myth of certainty. Contemplating the prospect of death brings immediacy to the present moment, and suddenly a very different reality can unfold. Through the process of further reflection, a greater awareness of death occurs and eventually a calm presence in the face of death can be developed. Many dying people quite spontaneously and naturally turn their focus away from worldly problems and become concerned instead with questions about the meaning and purpose of life—an investigation that can be inspirational as well as enlivening. As Stephen Levine says, "Many people say that they have never been so alive as at the time they are dying."[22]

For those physicians, nurses, loved ones, and friends who are able to remain open-minded and unafraid in the face of death, unusually strong bonds of love and understanding can develop between them and the person who is dying. Unfortunately, though, most people have not reflected on their own beliefs and fears about death, and for them it can be very difficult, if not impossible, to remain unguarded and open when interacting with a dying person. Fear and anxiety contaminate the exchange and can block the possibility of a real, heartfelt connection, especially when unexpected or unusual events occur. Although some people do not experience extraordinary events around death, many do, and it's therefore important to acknowledge the possibility of such occurrences and learn to accept them open-mindedly.

I had an extraordinary experience when Kazu, an elderly Japanese man, summoned me to his bedside just prior to his death. Kazu had cancer and was dying at home, surrounded by his loving family: a wife, two sisters, and four daughters. I visited him twice a week to assess pain medications, and to assist his family with

problems. Kazu and I developed an understanding that went beyond the daily routine of case management, and one day he told
me in a confidential whisper, "My time to die is soon." He also
said that he was afraid to leave because he did not want to disap-
point his wife and sisters who were constantly planning their future with him, and reminding him, "Next summer, Kazu, we go to
Vegas, yeah?"

Spontaneously, I whispered into Kazu's ear, "You call me when
it is time to go. I will hear you and come and help you." I immediately questioned in my own mind the sensibility of such a
promise. How could it happen? Kazu couldn't even use a phone.
Two days later, as I was turning into the parking lot of the Queen's
Hospital in Honolulu on my way to a 9:00 A.M. meeting, I dis-
tinctly heard a voice call out my name: "Margie." I considered it for
a moment but then chalked it up to stress or the fact that I really
didn't want to attend the meeting. Then I heard the voice again
and definitely felt it was Kazu's. I quickly changed course and drove
to his house. The women were very surprised to see me since I
wasn't scheduled to come that day. "How is Kazu?" I asked. "Oh,
fine," his wife replied, "he had some tea for breakfast."

I went to Kazu's bedside, where he lay with his eyes closed. He
seemed so tired, and he did not look at me, but softly squeezed
my hand as I slipped it into his. I lay my fingers gently across his
wrist. His pulse was faint and rapid. Softly I said, "Kazu, I heard
you calling me. I am here now. If you want to go it's all right; I will
help the women. It's okay if you want to leave." As I spoke, the
beats of his pulse became more erratic, and then they stopped. I
was completely shocked, dazed. He was gone! For several moments I thought about what role I might have played in his death
by encouraging him to leave. Then the sisters came up behind me
and asked how he was. Unable to register the profundity of what
had happened, I stalled for time, grasping for a way to prepare
them. I said, "He is getting weaker. I don't think he is doing well."
The two sisters began weeping, and then the other family members came into the room and stood clutching one another near the

door. His wife wailed, "Please don't die, Kazu. Oh, please don't leave us!" After about five long minutes, I said out loud, "Go in peace, Kazu; the women here all love you enough to allow you to go in peace. Hear how quiet the room is becoming." The crying diminished, and the women gathered themselves together with a noble dignity that suited their beloved Kazu. As each of us silently worked through the startling reality of death, we ritualized Kazu's passing by bathing his body with perfumed water and dressing him in some of his favorite clothes.

Experiences such as this one with Kazu remind me that beyond the so-called reality of ordinary thinking and mundane habit, a transcendent realm of inner experience exists and can also be known. Such inexplicable occurrences at the time of someone's death have taught me to maintain an open mind and a more accepting attitude. To ignore, discount, or pathologize unusual and mysterious events forecloses the door to deeper understanding. To remain open to them—and all inner callings—allows the healing process to unfold.

In my nursing practice I have either personally observed or heard about hundreds of events surrounding death that cannot be explained by conventional thinking—fleeting flashes of insight, brief moments of clear understanding so powerful that they alter the witness's point of view profoundly. I had such an experience when my best friend, Catherine, died.

Catherine had been in an automobile accident while we were in college that left her quadriplegic until the time that she died, ten years later. Throughout her long and often tortured life following the accident, Catherine cycled many times through the five stages of dying originally identified by Kübler-Ross: denial, anger, bargaining, depression, and acceptance. Fortunately, Catherine's family was able to provide her with all the required physical assistance that she needed: her parents added a huge suite and a handicap bathroom to their home and hired full-time attendants. Catherine lived there for several years while she struggled with the meaning of her newly imposed limitations. At her request I lived there too, commuting to nursing school in San Francisco. Five years later, after my husband and I had married and had our two children, we built a studio addition to our house in Aptos so that Catherine could stay with us, and when her physical condition was still strong, she came often.

A few years after her last visit, Catherine's brother called me one day to say that Catherine was "drifting away." I was startled and said, "What do you mean 'drifting away'?" He told me that the cancer she had developed in her bladder could no longer be contained or controlled by chemotherapy and that now she was slipping into unconsciousness. He also said that she had asked for me several times, and that I ought to come to see her right away. It was difficult for me to agree to go to her that night. It was a long drive, but really I was afraid of facing Catherine's death. I didn't know what I would say to her, and I did not want to see her die. What if she died right while I was there? What would I do? As a nurse I was supposed to know what to do around death, but, at that point, I didn't. I was unable to sleep that night and called Catherine's home early the next morning. Her brother answered the phone and told me that the mortuary had taken her body away just an hour ago. "She died?" I gasped. "I will be right there."

Driving across the Golden Gate Bridge to the mortuary, I remembered the wonderful apartment on Telegraph Hill that we had once shared with two other friends. We had all been in prep school together and had then become sorority sisters at UC Berkeley. Our social lives were focused on parties, clothes, and marriage. We never seriously considered that death would ever be part of our lives. Now, just ten years later, Catherine was dead. I wondered why I hadn't hurried to see her the night before while she was still alive, instead of rushing to see her now, when she was already gone.

Soon I was waiting nervously in a special room of the mortuary—Catherine's mother had given me permission to view the corpse. I heard the clanging of metal, and then the door opened and the mortician wheeled in the gurney holding Catherine's draped body. After he left, I cautiously lifted the sheet that covered her motionless face. Her eyes were half shut. They looked cloudy and dry. Her last breath seemed to linger, to hang almost audibly in the set of her mouth. I fought to keep from crying, and my throat constricted in pain. Leaning over and gazing at her, I saw tears from my eyes hit the blue-white granite of her cheek and smoothly roll, like raindrops down a statue, to the sheet below. I stood there transfixed.

Being with Catherine like that after she had died transported me to a space beyond the confines of my own conventional thinking. I realized that the pain gripping my chest as I looked at her corpse was the dark shadow of my own sense of loss. She, on the other hand, was finally free from physical boundaries and the paralysis that had kept her locked in one position for so long. I felt her presence in the room. She was there, I sensed, but no longer a part of the silent corpse that used to be Catherine. I kissed her ice-cold lips and thanked her for teaching me so much about friendship, love, and the uncertainty of life and its constant changes. Though deeply regretful for not having been physically present during Catherine's last moments, as I stood there observing her body after death, I felt graced with an amazingly clear view of the vastness of impermanence. I felt entirely connected and interrelated with everything. Past, future, death, and life were all present at once.

Although we deeply long for permanence, death teaches us with stunning clarity that it is nowhere to be found. When loved ones die, the passage of their physical presence from the world forces a reckoning with the inevitability of mortality and change. Time after time, reminders appear of what once was but is no longer—the deceased's pajamas lying behind the hamper, or a hat carelessly shoved to the back of the closet, or a note scribbled on a crumpled piece of paper. Yet the dead person is no longer materially in the world, no longer a physical presence in the stream of events. Death is both painful to acknowledge and difficult to accept, but it is also the natural and normal outcome of life. Death is the universally shared destiny of everything that lives and is the most powerful teacher of the uncertainty of life and the omnipresence of impermanence. If we can courageously open ourselves to these truths, we can eventually develop a lasting sense of peace—and, most importantly, we can be of real assistance to others.

3

Awakening to Impermanence and Facing Death

Like scientists, if we discover upon examination that certain states of mind are unwholesome in that they bring us suffering and problems, then we should realize the significance of this insight and seek a way to eradicate them.

—TENZIN GYATSO, THE FOURTEENTH DALAI LAMA, *The World of Tibetan Buddhism*

I DEVELOPED A LASTING AWARENESS ABOUT the uncertainty of life working as a nurse in a large emergency center—a place that continually trembled with change and unpredictability. Many of the patients had sustained either a shocking injury or the rapid onset of illness, which caused a sudden loss of their sense of safety and security. Flimsy, stained curtains provided the only semblance of privacy between the beds as patient after patient arrived, each presenting a problem that required immediate intervention. Some would leave the emergency area stabilized; others simply died. Never knowing what kind of dramatic shock might occur next, I began to have glimpses of the utter transitoriness of the body and, for that matter, all aspects of life. Frightened by my growing awareness of the tenuousness of life, I tried to maintain a personal sense of security by perceiving my "real" world as separate from my work world. I believed that the events happening to other people in the emergency room had nothing to do with me.

Most of us who worked in the emergency room were galvanized by the constantly urgent energy there, yet we were also frequently challenged by the deluge of tragedies that occurred. Some of us became very proficient at shielding ourselves from emotional pain. We could perform emergency care almost devoid of any empathetical connection with the patient. Of course, it is always important to function objectively when responding to a crisis, but focusing solely on skills and efficiency also fostered a certain coldheartedness toward the patient as an individual. For example, it was a common practice among the caregivers to carry on superficial and meaningless conversations with each other while carrying out procedures and treatments for patients. A patient would be addressed when necessary with rote instructions: "Don't move now, I am going to put a tube down your nose into your stomach. Hold your breath and swallow."

When I first started practicing in the emergency room I was shocked to hear a nurse say, "I feel nothing for these people, and that is how I can deal with working here." I thought such an attitude was selfish and the person who expressed it, heartless. But after several months of experiencing the intense emotions that arose in many of the crises that unfolded, I too began to psychologically distance myself from the patients. In my mind, they gradually lost their individuality and became a separate category of beings with a problem that would be diagnosed and treated. Then they left. I usually never saw the same patient again. The longer I worked there, the less inclined I was to feel empathy. Once in a while a particularly painful death—a small child beaten to death by an abusive parent, a pregnant teenager stabbed to death by a jealous lover—would arouse tremendous rage and indignation among all of us in the emergency room; yet I can still vividly recall the naive sense of separateness I felt, until one day when my limited point of view was dramatically shaken.

It started out as an ordinary morning. I had driven from Santa Monica to downtown Los Angeles, where the sun's light was pushing against the thick smog that blanketed the skyline. Holding a cup of coffee, I walked into the emergency room and sat down with the other day nurses and physicians to listen to the night nurses' report on the patients who were in the department. Most patients had been treated and released during the night, except for two "tagged and bagged" bodies that awaited transport to the morgue; they were at the moment hidden away from view on two stretchers in the shower room. After the morning report, each nurse picked the treatment area that he or she would be responsible for during that shift. I drew the trauma room that was reserved for critical injuries or other extreme emergencies, and it had been empty for two hours. Ambulatory patients were arriving from the walk-in triage area, and paramedics wheeled in patients on stretchers through the ambulance entrance. I checked the emergency carts and swabbed down the counters with alcohol while I waited for a patient to be admitted to the trauma room.

I didn't wait for long. The paramedics wheeled in Bill. He was sitting with his back propped up against the stretcher. An old, worn-out ambulance sheet was crumpled behind him and hanging off the much-used black vinyl mattress. Bill was about forty years old, and his large frame completely filled the stretcher. He had on running shoes with no socks and a pair of wrinkled khaki pants. Bill had been shot in the chest with an arrow. The paramedics had cut off his shirt, leaving his chest bare except for the slender, feathered shaft protruding from it. Pointing at his sternum, Bill asked over and over, with a perplexed and pained look on his face, "Man oh man, how was I to know Frank was comin' home?" Bill was in no acute distress, but his X rays showed the

47

arrowhead to be lodged deeply in his chest wall; it would have to be removed surgically. He would stay in the trauma room for observation until an operating room was available. Several policemen on their way out of the department stopped at the doorway and looked in at him. Grinning, they shook their heads in disbelief. Bill said to them, "How was I to know Frank was comin' home? An arrow, man, an *arrow*. If I'da only knew Frank shot arrows, man, ohhh man." Then, after drifting off for a moment, he whistled and said, "It was worth it though, man, it was *worth* it. Whoo-*whee*, talk about the *love'* goddess, man." I could hear the policemen laughing as one of them said, "Isn't that the damnedest thing you ever saw? I'd be real embarrassed if somethin' like that happened to me."

Shandra, the other patient the paramedics had brought into the trauma room, had temporary paralysis in both legs and a cardiac arrhythmia brought about by a severe potassium deficiency. She had not been taking her prescribed potassium replacement, since she had used up all her money to buy food. Shandra was responding rapidly to an intravenous infusion of fluids and electrolytes that the paramedics had started earlier. She lay with her head turned to the side and was staring at the arrow in Bill's chest. I was considering myself lucky, since both cases were very easy and would be occupying the trauma room for hours. The head nurse notified the paramedics that we were closed to further critical admissions until my two patients were stable and transferred out of the trauma room. Then I heard the ward clerk yell in to me, "Coberly, phone call, line three." I walked to a phone on the wall, picked up the receiver and punched in the flashing button. It was my brother, Wheeler.

"Marg," he said, his voice charged with urgency, "the biopsy is back, and the doctor says that it is malignant. But they won't know how bad it is until they go in and look. He wants to do a mini-thoracotomy on Thursday." I was aghast. In an astonishingly swift turn, the world suddenly felt very unsafe. The walls of the room seemed to loom around me like ominous, ugly barriers as I watched the second hand on the huge clock move forward, stop briefly, then backtrack before clicking onward. In the background I could hear Bill talking to a visitor at his bedside, "Now I know about the *love* goddess, man, Eros, '*ar*-rows,' get it, man? You understand what I am sayin', man? Whoo-*wheeeee!*" Shandra, completely responsive now, was asking the volunteer, "Is that really an arrow?" I could see myself reflected in the shiny paper towel dispenser next to the phone cradle on the wall. Mascara was smeared under one of my eyes, and I looked scared. I did not know what to say to Wheeler. I could only envision the emergency thoracotomies I had seen, the deep incision through the superficial layers of the chest wall, the huge retractors used to pull apart the ribs and expose the organs beneath, and the blood. There was always so much blood draining everywhere when a chest was "cracked" in the trauma room.

"What's a *mini*-thoracotomy?" I asked him as I tried to make sense of his words in the midst of my intense visceral reaction to what he was saying.

"You should know that!" he snapped at me. "The doctor said that he would make an incision above the nipple and look around in there, but I will only be in the hospital for two days."

"What kind of cancer do they think it is?" I asked, cautiously.

"They don't know yet, but if it's Hodgkin's disease it is very curable. Pray for Hodgkin's disease, all right? Pray for Hodgkin's. Will you be with me on Thursday?"

"Of course I will," I said.

I hung up the phone and terror washed over me. It seemed impossible that Wheeler could have cancer. What if he died? He was only forty-nine years old, and although his two daughters were grown up he had recently begun a new family with his second wife. I said over and over to myself, "I will not pray for Hodgkin's disease, I will not do it." Looking at the feathered end of the arrow sticking out of Bill's chest, I thought about how close he had come to death this morning, and Shandra too. She could have died, with her potassium level as perilously low as it had been. I had done what was necessary to carry out the physician's orders for both Bill and Shandra, but I had not felt their pain. I had not put myself in their shoes. In fact, in my mind I had labeled them "easy patients" and indifferently shrugged off their circumstances. Now, quite suddenly, I was experiencing my own personal fear of loss and death: it made the patients seem more real to me.

Many of the conditioned beliefs I held about myself as an aloof nurse, capable of maintaining a necessary and appropriate distance from a patient, suddenly seemed useless. This time, dying was happening to someone I could not distance myself from. This time a confrontation with my own fear of death was unavoidable; I would have to respond to terminal illness and death at a much deeper level than I was prepared for. I looked around and saw the desperate circumstances that were enveloping people, all at the same time, just in that one emergency room. I thought about the thousands of other emergency rooms that were probably overflowing with patients in transition, with families in crisis, with lives hovering in the shadows of death. And I realized how fragile life actually is.

Death's Scythe

Coming face-to-face with mortality and impending loss is an intense, poignant experience, and I was encountering it firsthand as I sat in the small waiting room adjacent to the surgical suites where my brother was having his operation. It was Thursday morning, and the physicians were about to cut through Wheeler's chest wall and explore his thoracic cavity to determine the extent of the cancer tumor that was growing there. I hoped they would be able to remove all the malignant cells and render him cancer-free, but I felt dread and foreboding, and I sensed that my reality was being irreversibly altered. The heavy double doors into the operating area would occasionally open as a stretcher was pushed in or out, and I could see down the wide hall where hospital personnel in green scrubs, booties, and paper shower caps were carrying trays of instruments and pushing carts full of supplies. My brother was in there somewhere. To the hospital staff he was just another anonymous patient, draped and anesthetized. I could picture him lying on the operating room table with the end of an endotracheal tube taped to his mouth and his thoracic cavity cut open. I thumbed through magazines and restlessly sipped coffee as I tried to disregard the treacherous questions that endlessly circled through my mind: What if the cancer has spread? What if he dies? Is there a cure? What are his chances? Could it be a mistake? What if the doctors are wrong?

In my mind, I kept seeing the troubled faces of patients I had known who had endured the grueling treatments prescribed for cancer. Some survived; many didn't. Every hospital I had ever been in had its share of haunted corridors where the dying passed by on their way to and from radiation or chemotherapy. Most of them had lost their hair and they had thin, emaciated bodies and expressionless faces. "Is it really worth it?" I would often ask myself. "What would I do if I had cancer?" So many people respond to a terminal diagnosis with the sweeping proclamation, "I am going to beat this if it is the last thing I do." That would probably be my first response, too. Or I might want only alternative therapies—prayer, visualization, meditation, stress reduction, nutritional support, massage, life-style change—and rather than fight, use my energy to develop inner peace. Or maybe I would choose to have no treatment at all, but instead go out and do everything I always wanted to do. But in that case what about the pain? And who would take care of me? Besides, wasn't that giving up? But giving up what?

I was imagining many scenarios as I leaned against the wall in one of the gray upholstered chairs that lined the waiting room. My mother sat next to me. She was reading, her glasses resting half way down her nose. I thought, "How terrible to lose an only son and the hero of the family. What kind of justice is there in that?" Wheeler's beautiful wife, Maggie, sat next to me on the other side. She and Wheeler had had two sons, one eight years old and the other three. What would Maggie do if Wheeler died? Abandoned, bereft, she would have to raise the boys alone. Next to her sat Wheeler's closest friend, John. His face was swollen and red, side effects from the medications he had to take in order to prevent a rejection of his recent kidney transplant. He and Wheeler had both been so strong and healthy in college. What happened? How had I come to believe that sickness and suffering only occur in other people's lives? Looking at the faces of everyone in that waiting room, I knew I was not the only one in pain there. But no one said anything.

Finally Wheeler's primary surgeon, the pulmonologist, strode into the waiting room. A surgical cap lay askew on his head and his shoes were wrapped in green paper booties that matched his rumpled scrub suit. The mask that had covered his mouth during surgery was now hanging limply from his neck. His voice had control and firmness in it, but his words lacked conviction. "The cancer is growing from the thymus area and is wrapped around the aorta," he announced. "It is far too extensive for us to remove. But it does not mean he is a goner; we have many different kinds of chemotherapy treatments. The type of cancer cell it is will determine the choice of agents to be used, and we won't know that until the tissue analysis is back in a few days."

We all crowded around the doctor. We wanted more answers than he was able to give, and our questions were tinged with a rising hysteria. I pondered his use of the word "goner," wondering if that word had been used in the operating room when they'd seen the extent of the metastasis. We used "goner" a lot in the emergency room: "If we can't stop the bleeding, this one is a goner," or "We can save him now, but tomorrow he'll probably be a goner," or "Call the code, she's a goner." The doctor backed away from us, saying only, "He will be out of recovery and back in his room in a few hours. You can see him then."

We began talking to each other cautiously, nervously, about

what to do next, what to say to Wheeler, which oncologist to seek for treatment, what kind of treatment would work. But none of us really knew any answers, and we each had the silent, aching knowledge that a catastrophe was happening in our lives. As unprepared as I was for such an event, I was full of wildly contradictory thoughts and overcome with excruciating emotional pain, and everyone else seemed equally confused and upset. I thought to myself that I would do anything, anything at all to change the circumstances back to the way they were before, to stop the clock and reverse the doom that appeared to lie ahead. We had to keep up appearances for Wheeler, and above all we had to protect him and ourselves from contemplating the terrifying possibility that he might actually die.

Receiving a terminal diagnosis forces us into an awkward and unwelcome encounter with death—a disorienting event for everyone concerned. Most of us know only avoidance and denial strategies, and so we feel clumsy and helpless when facing death. I was not only Wheeler's sister but also his nurse: thus I was forced to face his impending death all day, every day. There was no way to escape. To be of any real help to him and to the family, I had to find a way to understand what was happening. I knew that a very strong antidote was needed if I was going to overcome my own death-denial. When I thought about losing Wheeler, a cold, tight fist would harden in my chest. It was just too painful to imagine life without him. Even more excruciating was the habitual belief I had that any death meant a complete and everlasting break with the person who died. How was I going to be able to face it? Would I ever understand it, or accept it? It did not seem possible.

During the weeks and months that followed Wheeler's initial diagnosis, I learned that ongoing courage would be required to face death and dying, and I needed to find a way to develop that courage. I had heard of several inspired teachers—Elisabeth Kübler-Ross, Stephen Levine, and Ram Dass—and I eagerly read their views on death, dying, caring, and healing. Their observations and advice broadened my point of view and also introduced me generally to the wisdom of the East. Around the same time, I happened to pick up a book on Tibetan Buddhism while browsing at the bookstore. Encountering these ideas began to give me a new frame of reference. Over time, these teachings helped me to live each day more fully and completely, "to take the time *that day*," as Elisabeth Kübler-Ross writes, "to become more of who you really are, to reach out to other human beings."[1]

In the Tibetan Buddhist view, which I will present more fully in Part Two, dying is not conceived of as a tragic end, but as a natural and very special process—one that when properly understood can become an extraordinary opportunity for spiritual development. Dying is said to unfold in a series of stages, each with its own milestones and possibilities, and what we in the West call the final "end" is not seen as such in Tibetan Buddhism. In their view, life follows death just as death follows life, and rebirth occurs—whether we believe in it or not. This concept of continuation and rebirth was a radical departure from what I was conditioned to believe. It offered a whole new way for me to intellectually understand death and at the same time it gave me a glimmer of hope that made my aching heart rejoice. Not only was the idea of rebirth comforting, it also produced an awareness of possible realities beyond the space and time limits of the conventional world, beyond the confines of the ordinary mind.

I found Tibetan Buddhism surprisingly straightforward. The texts were easy for me to read, and as a result I rapidly gained valuable new insights. Soon it was less difficult to be comfortable with Wheeler. And, as I slowly opened to receiving some of death's deeper lessons and mysteries, it became increasingly easy to just allow the silences to quietly fill the room in their own way.

One day Wheeler asked me, "Listen, hear that? Hear that owl?" He had mentioned the owls several times before, but I had never been able to hear them. He had insisted that owls were living nearby and that they were going to escort him when he died. Wheeler lived in Brentwood, California, a dense urban area in southern California, and even though there were many eucalyptus trees around, I couldn't imagine owls living there. Suddenly, though, I heard them too. They hooted every night outside the bedroom window. I heard them hooting right when Wheeler's breathing stopped, and I heard them hooting as the morticians were zipping the vinyl bag around his body. And I heard them again as Wheeler's wife, Maggie, and I clung to each other and watched as two men from the mortuary preceded us up the stairs and struggled with Wheeler's stiff body as they tried to round the corner at the landing. We slowly followed, watching them cross the living room and walk out the front door into the black night. As the men loaded Wheeler's body into their van, we all heard the owls hooting around the house.

Wheeler's friend Tom had agreed to drive me behind the van as it wound its way down the hill toward the mortuary. I had promised Wheeler that I would stay with him for as long as I was allowed to. When we reached the place where his body would be refrigerated prior to cremation, the two men opened the back of the van, positioned their gurney, and then slid his body onto it. As they passed by us I softly whispered, "Good-bye, my most beloved brother, and you were so right about the owls! I will never forget you." Then the men pushed the gurney through a heavy metal door and disappeared. He was gone. The next night, Maggie and I sat in the downstairs bedroom for a while and talked about Wheeler. The room felt very empty, even though his presence strongly remained. Then we noticed that the owls were no longer hooting. We soon realized that they had indeed gone, just as suddenly as they had appeared.

It was with the greatest wonder and appreciation that Wheeler's grieving daughters heard us tell the story of the owls. And it elicited a powerful sense of reconnection between them and their dead father, especially as they began to remember having heard the owls themselves. If Wheeler had not told me about the owls, I wonder if Maggie or I would have noticed them at all, but when we did, the Tibetan Buddhist texts became even more real to me as I contemplated the possibility of connections and meanings that were deeper than I had ever experienced.

Two weeks before Wheeler died, he had asked me for an injection of morphine strong enough to kill him. It wasn't difficult for me to understand why he wanted to end his life: his body had become like a skeleton with loose dry skin hanging from it, and he could do nothing more than drift in and out of sleep. He was in a lot of pain, even though he was taking the maximum amount of narcotics the physician would allow. The last time Wheeler had been out of bed, he had almost collapsed in the shower. His hands and feet had turned a deep blue as Maggie and I struggled to hold him up. Later that night he had cried in embarrassment for his dependency and for putting such a "heavy burden" on us. It was extremely painful for us to see him suffer so deeply, and very frustrating to be unable to help. But there was no possibility in my mind, at all, that I would or could give him a lethal dose of morphine, regardless how many times he asked.

At night I slept on a cot near his bed, and almost every hour his hoarse whisper would awaken me with a request for pain medicine. I gave him as much as I could. The tumor over his aorta bulged menacingly from his chest, and he groaned when he had to move. He would often complain despondently about his inability to "let go and get out" of his body. One afternoon, as I was wiping his face with a washcloth, he looked at me with tear-filled eyes and pleaded, "Please help me, Marg, please." His tormented face made my heart wrench. I touched his forehead and told him how sorry I was that he had to suffer, but said that I could not give him an overdose.

Later that evening I went upstairs for dinner. When I came back, Wheeler was lying facedown on the carpet, about four feet from the bed. I was astonished. He had barely moved at all for several days. I rushed over to him and checked to see if he was breathing. "Wheeler, Wheeler," I said, "you are facedown on the carpet! How did this happen?" I heard him whispering into the carpet, "Got to go, got to get out." Maggie called a friend of

Wheeler's who lived a few houses away. He came running over and helped us carry Wheeler back to bed. When we turned him over onto his back and began to lift him, we saw the imprint of the table on his chest. It appeared as though he had flung himself against its corner, striking his chest with full force. The tumor looked even more malformed now, with the table stamped into it like that. I felt very sad and angry with myself that Wheeler had had to resort to such action because he couldn't get help any other way.

Over the next few hours his pulse weakened and faded, and even though he was propped straight up on many pillows, he could barely inhale. I told him that it was time for him to go. "Head toward the brightest light you can see," I said. "Don't be afraid of it." He remained responsive to the very end, looking frightened one moment and jubilant the next. I continued to urge him softly onward, and gently sprayed oxygen around his face. He took his last breaths in three short, rapid gasps. Then his heart stopped beating and he lay there lifeless, staring out at us with fixed and dilated pupils.

The remarkable silence that fills the room when someone dies is stunning, and it can feel overpoweringly empty and frightening when viewed from a perspective of death denial. But when Wheeler died, even though I felt excruciatingly sad, the silence was charged with possibilities and was infinitely beautiful. The pain of seeing his body there unmoving, so still and lifeless, was wrenching. But was that really still Wheeler? That corpse lying there greatly resembled him, but he was not present in it. Tears welled up in my eyes when I thought of my world without him and the world of his wife and family without him, but I held them back as much as I could and tried to heed the words of the great Tibetan teachers I had read. According to them, a person who has just stopped breathing needs our help more than ever to avoid being distracted from a forward move along the path after death, and our uncontained sorrows can be a powerful disruption. The shell of Wheeler—that skeletal form of loosely held-together bones—had sunk heavily into the pillows. Death had arrived, but where was it? Didn't Wheeler still feel absolutely present there somehow? Weren't we connected now in some ineffable way? Wasn't the part of me observing death precisely the same thing that had just departed from his body? In spite of the achingly heavy sense of loss that I felt, the Tibetan Buddhist teachings suddenly sprang to life: death can be understood and acknowledged as life's greatest teacher. It brings new awareness—a shift in priorities.

Questioning Assumptions

In the Tibetan Buddhist tradition, a careful and continual analysis of death and the way it alters our beliefs about permanence is necessary to develop an unwavering appreciation of life. Tibetan Buddhism advocates confronting personal mortality and cultivating an awareness of impermanence moment to moment, because through such contemplation a person can gain true understanding about the tenuous quality of life, and the fleeting nature of everything except the essence of the mind (more on this in Part Two). To gain such understanding can ease some of the pain we feel when death collides with our future. The idea that any one of us could die at any moment changes our priorities. In a terminal illness the shock of that first terse knowing—that moment when all expectations are suddenly suspended—can catapult a person into another state of awareness.

When my cousin Cobe died it completely traumatized the entire family. He died at home with his sons and wife at his bedside. By the time I arrived, his body had already been taken to the mortuary, although his presence still remained very strong throughout the house. I saw his slippers lying askew by the door where he had left them. His water glass on the bedside table still had the faint outline of his lips on its rim. The impermanence of life was evident everywhere and infused the air with wonder and awe; it also brought a sense of vast, unspeakable loss. I thought about a conversation I had had with him a year or so earlier, right after he was diagnosed with the terminal illness. His voice had sounded so animated and elated. It wasn't joy for having a potentially lethal disease, but joy for suddenly seeing life from an entirely new perspective—a larger and more panoramic framework than the one conditioned by his past experience. Suddenly he had been able to let go of many preconceived ideas he had about himself, about who he was and what his father wanted him to be. It was as if the shadow of death allowed him to think of life in a new way.

I went with Cobe's sons, Bud and Sterling, to the mortuary to complete the paperwork and plan for the cremation. Mr. Bornthorpe, the mortician, sat behind his desk and peered at us over the top of his magnifying glasses. "What type of box do you wish to purchase for Mr. Coberly's transport to the crematorium?" he asked. None of us knew what the procedure was at a mortuary, and neither Bud nor Sterling had been advised in any earlier conversations that a box would have to be purchased. Mr. Bornthorpe reached into his bookcase, pulled out a huge three-ring binder, and began to tap on it as he explained some of the state laws regarding death.

"Any body that is slated for cremation must be transported to the crematorium in a box that is big enough to hold the body," he said, "yet small enough to fit inside the burning chamber." We looked at him in horror and then looked at each other in disbelief. It was difficult to understand how Mr. Bornthorpe could be so unfeeling and cold. He went on to explain that there were several different styles and options to choose from, and that most were readily available. Leafing through the pages of the binder, he showed us illustrations of the boxes, from the least expensive, made of corrugated cardboard, to the most expensive, made of hardwood and boasting gold-plated hinges. None of us had slept all night, and Bud and Sterling were numb with disbelief that their dad had actually died. They had known that death was approaching, but like almost everyone else, they had never expected it would arrive so soon. It seemed ludicrous that at such a time they should have to sit like captives in Mr. Bornthorpe's office listening to a sales pitch for crematorium boxes as a sentimental dirge wafted in from the gilded chapel area in front.

Finally Mr. Bornthorpe rose from his desk and beckoned us to follow him into the casket room. He flipped up two switches on the wall by the entrance, and the room became flooded with fluorescent light and the sound of canned organ music. We looked at some of the different caskets. One was propped open. It was made of cherry wood and had a pink satin lining. A price tag dangled from one of the hinges: $18,000.

"Dad would be so pissed if he knew we were spending thousands of dollars on a box that is just going to be burned up," Bud said pragmatically.

"He's not going down in a cardboard box," snapped Sterling.

"Let's build the box ourselves," I suggested.

"Do you know how?" Bud asked. And they both wondered out loud, "Is that normal?"

"Why not?" I said.

I thought about the way our fatigue and grief had begun to make us vulnerable to the mortician's prodding suggestion that a family's respect for the deceased is measured by the amount of money they are willing to spend on the funeral. For some people it might be so. Respect for the dead comes in diverse forms in America. Among Tibetan Buddhists, respect for the deceased is defined in various ways, too. For example, a ceremony called "sky burial" is sometimes carried out, especially in the more stark areas of Tibet where the environment is harsh and there are few resources. In sky burial, the body of the deceased is cut into pieces, rolled in grain, and respectfully offered to the birds. This is seen as a last act of extreme generosity on the part of the person who has died. Thinking about sky burial made the falsity of the funeral parlor seem very superficial indeed. We left there with firm resolve: I would draw the plans according to the measurements that Mr. Bornthorpe provided, and then we would make the box.

Later we drove to a lumber yard and bought wood, hinges, latches, nails, screws, putty, glue, and varnish, and then spent the rest of the day building the box. As other relatives and friends arrived at the house, they gathered around the project some pitching in, others watching. As the box slowly took shape, it became a central point of interest and focused people's grief on a constructive outcome. It also helped Bud and Sterling overcome the sense of helplessness that had been enveloping them since their dad had died.

The following morning we delivered the beautifully varnished box to the mortuary for Mr. Bornthorpe to use to transport Cobe's body to the crematorium. "Look at that," Mr. Bornthorpe marveled, "You even varnished the inside!" Before the box was carried away, both Cobe's wife and his sister ceremoniously and lovingly placed some of his most treasured things in it, and then said their final good-byes. Building the box and driving it to the mortuary was an experience that unified us all. It was gratifying for almost everyone, even those who initially thought that such an approach might not be appropriate. We all felt very close to one another for having joined forces in such a constructive way.

My study of Tibetan Buddhism has helped me to remain open-minded and calm in the face of death, and allowed me to respond more creatively to many of the situations that arise during a dying trajectory. Two Tibetan teachings have been of particular help to me in working with terminally ill people and their families. One is a death meditation; the other is a description of the eight stages of dissolution that lead up to death. These two teachings, even though imbedded in a much larger system, have great potential, on their own, to help a person understand death from a broadened perspective. In order to understand them, however, some knowledge about basic Buddhist concepts is required. Therefore, the following chapter will present a brief overview of Tibetan Buddhist thought.

Although I have found aspects of Tibetan Buddhism especially helpful in my own professional practice, my intent is not to put these forward as necessarily more appropriate than other approaches, and certainly not to suggest them for everyone. In fact, a broader view of healing would be wedded to no one particular psychospiritual path or methodology. The Tibetan Buddhist literature on death and dying is vast, and in the chapters that follow I draw upon only selected English-language resources that I think are especially useful, either because they contain concrete applications that can be adapted by Westerners, or because they can provide real insights about the meaning of life, death, and dying.

PART TWO

RESOURCES FROM THE TIBETAN BUDDHIST TRADITION

As when with downcast eyes we muse and brood,
And ebb into a former life, or seem
To lapse far back in a confusèd dream
To states of mystical similitude,
If one but speaks or hems or stirs his chair
Ever the wonder waxeth more and more,
So that we say, "All this hath been before,
All this hath been, I know not when or where."

ALFRED, LORD TENNYSON, Sonnet I

4

Ceaseless Transformation

> *Every major religion of the world—Buddhism,*
> *Christianity, Confucianism, Hinduism, Islam,*
> *Jainism, Judaism, Sikhism, Taoism, Zoroastri-*
> *anism—has similar ideals of love, the same goal*
> *of benefiting humanity through spiritual*
> *practice, and the same effect of making their*
> *followers into better human beings.*
>
> —Tenzin Gyatso, the Fourteenth
> Dalai Lama, *Ocean of Wisdom*

BUDDHISM IS BASED ON THE LIFE AND teachings of Siddhartha Gautama, a man who lived in India in the fifth century B.C.E. and came to be known as the Buddha or "Awakened One." Like Jesus or Moses, the Buddha was an extraordinary spiritual teacher who offered great wisdom and insight into the meaning and purpose of human existence. In the centuries following the Buddha's death, his teachings spread throughout the Asian world—to China, Sri Lanka, Japan, Tibet, Korea, Thailand, Vietnam, Cambodia—and eventually to the

West. As Buddhism spread, various schools developed that emphasized different elements of the Buddha's teaching, and Buddhist philosophy and practice evolved as it interacted with the cultures of different countries and regions. In the eighth century, Buddhism moved into Tibet, the mountainous region to the northeast of India, and began to develop in its own way there as it interacted with Tibetan culture and indigenous beliefs.

Many care providers would like to increase their knowledge and understanding about death and thereby become more compassionate and helpful caregivers to the dying. Tibetan Buddhism offers many powerful and coherent teachings about life and death that can be extremely helpful in overcoming the fear that arises when facing a dying person. At first glance many of these teachings may seem dauntingly unfamiliar. Yet the Tibetan Buddhist perspective is worth exploring in some detail, since it provides a complete and practical framework for understanding life, death, and the process of dying. While several of these concepts may challenge your existing beliefs, it is important to consider these new ideas with an open mind, since they offer an outstanding opportunity to deepen both personal and transpersonal knowledge about death and the process of dying.

Dependent Origination: The Truth of Impermanence

Whatever is born is impermanent and is bound to die.
Whatever is stored is impermanent and is bound to run out.
Whatever is joined is impermanent and is bound to come apart.
Whatever is built is impermanent and is bound to collapse.
Whatever goes up is impermanent and is bound to fall down. [1]

In the Buddhist view, hoping and longing for permanence is futile, because permanence is impossible—impossible because everything is made up of parts, each dependent on the other, and all subject to change. Even though something appears as a single and discrete entity—solid, stable, and permanent—it originated from and now exists in dependence upon the sum of its parts. Take, for instance, a large boulder—heavy, ancient, and seemingly permanent. The appearance of the boulder is largely determined by the climatic forces that erode it—the wind and rain that wear away its surface and the endless temperature changes that open up and widen its cracks. The boulder is not only defined by its elemental composition, but by the combination of forces perpetually acting upon it. Eventually the boulder will erode away completely; it will become dust, each particle carrying on its own existence under the influence of its environment. This concept of dependent origination can be applied to any kind of perceived event or object. Ultimately, all matter is like a cloud, for example, outlined against the sky. The cloud appears solid yet is constantly in flux as the elements that compose it shift and change and then disperse altogether.

Dependent origination is unmistakably evident during the dying process as the elements that compose the body fade and dissolve during the final stages that lead to death. A person who is able to recognize dependent origination will also see the truth of impermanence everywhere. Such awareness has the psychological potential to evoke a remarkable shift in priorities. To understand now that all of the concerns of worldly life—the places, objects, people and ideas—are by their very nature only temporary, strengthens our acceptance and resilience later when those concerns actually do change or are lost. At death all concerns will fade and "dissolve in our tightest grasp," in the moving words of Robert A. F. Thurman, "forgotten if they were in our mind, lost if they were in our hand, faded into blank numbness if they were our mind and body."[2]

The search for permanence in a world that cannot provide it is a constant source of disappointment for people. Yet the compulsion to believe in permanence remains powerful in us and continually generates a strong sense of identification with the body, and a feeling of solidity and stability. The mind that believes in permanence is bound by the limits and needs of the body and is constantly preoccupied with the search for personal pleasure. As the mind strives in this way, it is filled with self-centered thoughts, such as "If so-and-so doesn't love me, I will be miserable," or "When I have more money, then I will be content," or "I can't be happy until they accept me." On the surface these thoughts appear as if they are based in fact. When examined more deeply, however, they can be seen as the unreliable fabrications that they really are—illusions that have been carefully crafted in an attempt to satisfy the senses. The Buddha said, "Do not aim at pleasure because the loss of pleasure is hell. Not ever grasping at pleasure, you will never be bound by its chains."[3]

At one time or another, most of us have experienced some degree of struggle and pain as a result of striving for physical and emotional fulfillment. Take, for example, the anguish that can result from developing a deep attachment in a romantic relationship. Often much time is spent preoccupied with thoughts of the beloved, who operates as the source of our deepest sensory pleasure and imagined long-term happiness. Yet the more dependence develops, the greater the attachment grows, and as a result the fear of losing the beloved creates negative forces in the mind such as jealousy, greed, anger, and pride. These dark thoughts create confusion and poor judgment and undermine the positive tendencies that are necessary for happiness in the relationship.

Karma: Form and Shadow Remain Linked

When the eagle soars up, high above the earth,
Its shadow for the while is nowhere to be seen;
Yet bird and shadow still are linked. So too our actions:
When conditions come together, their effects are clearly seen.[4]

Buddhists believe that all universes are dominated by the natural law of *karma*: for every action, or cause, there is a necessary and concordant reaction, or effect. In the Buddha's words, "Just as iron is eaten away by the rust it produces, so do your own wrong actions lead you to destruction."[5] Whether negative, positive, or neutral, every action makes a karmic imprint on us and creates the tendency to act in that same way again—both now and in the future. As Lama Yeshe says, "Once you've created the karma to experience a certain result, that's where you're headed."[6] Even when the direct effect of certain actions is not immediately evident, results will eventually occur.

In the Buddhist view, each of us is responsible for our own actions, and we alone reap their consequences. Since actions and deeds of the past strongly determine present circumstances, and actions taken today greatly influence the future, individuals have the unique opportunity to change and reshape their own happiness from one moment to the next. Each new moment presents the individual with a fresh chance to transcend latent negative tendencies and choose positive responses instead. There is an old Tibetan saying: if you want to know your past, examine your present circumstances; if you want to know your future, examine your present thinking.

Human survival depends on mutual cooperation among people, and a great sense of inner happiness can result from working for the welfare of others and the common good. In Buddhism the altruistic intention to work for the benefit of others, rather than just for oneself, is called *bodhichitta*.[7] Bodhichitta arises out of the awareness that all beings are equal in their wish to be happy and not to suffer. In the mind that is awakening to bodhichitta, a self-centered regard for oneself is slowly replaced with genuine compassion for others. Tibetan Buddhism maintains that every effort individuals make to restructure their lives to respond appropriately to the needs of others will predispose them to act in that same way again, and improve the condition of their mind.

The Dalai Lama says, "Even if we do not fully develop the awakening mind, because of its altruistic and all-pervasive frame of reference, we shall certainly become a kinder human being."[8]

Ordinary Mind: The Worlds We Find Ourselves In

The worlds we find ourselves in are not separate from us but arise from our own mental imprints.[9]

According to Tibetan Buddhist psychology, our entire mental potential—all conscious thought—falls into one of two categories: unenlightened and enlightened. The unenlightened mind is ordinary and conventional—it is superficial, limited by rote habits and customary beliefs, such as our attachments to permanence, stability, and personal comfort and pleasure. Most of us are dominated by this mind. The enlightened mind is totally open—free of bias or judgment—and perceives things as they truly are. Buddhists believe that an enlightened mind lies deep within the heart of every person and constitutes the fundamental nature of a human being. The most subtle form of this enlightened mind is said to never be extinguished; instead it passes from one lifetime to the next. This will be discussed in more detail later.

Unfortunately, most of us are fundamentally ignorant about the true capacity of our own mind; we tend to believe that it is bound by the body and limited to this one life. So even though we have the capacity to access the natural and impartial mind of enlightenment, our conventional thoughts and beliefs obscure it. In addition, Tibetan Buddhism teaches about four specific deterrents to recognizing the enlightened nature of mind, the "four faults":

1. In the same way that it is difficult to know the precise expression on one's own face, the true nature of the mind is *too close* to be recognized.

2. In the same way that it is difficult to comprehend the depth of the ocean, the profound capacity of the mind is *too deep* to fathom.

3. The capacity that a mind has to rest in its own nature of enlightenment seems *too easy*.

4. The potential for enlightenment does not fit within the narrow limits imposed by the ordinary mind and is therefore seemingly *too excellent* to be accommodated.[10]

Despite the four faults and the other barriers imposed by the ordinary mind, individuals have the capacity to expand their awareness and achieve enlightenment. From the Tibetan Buddhist perspective, even the most ordinary event can guide and nurture a person toward deeper understanding, because every image and thought that touches the senses has greater meaning than its conventional definition alone. In the end, the true essence of the mind is the only enduring asset that a person really ever has. The capacity of the human mind to gain self-knowledge, and recognize its essential nature, is extraordinarily significant and of central importance in Tibetan Buddhist psychology.

Enlightened Mind: The Light Within

One single torch can dissipate the accumulated darkness of a thousand eons. Likewise, one single instant of clear light in mind eliminates the ignorance and obscurations accumulated over kalpas.[11]

An enlightened mind, one that recognizes its own luminescence, is a potential source of perfect wisdom and happiness that is within each of us. The true nature of the mind is often described as clear light. In the Tibetan Buddhist view, the clear light of mind is a thread of continuity that streams through life and continues on after death. This clear light permeates every cell of the body and has the ability to separate from the body at death. In the words of the fourteenth Dalai Lama, "Just as oil penetrates the entire sesame seed, the essential nature of clear light penetrates every experience of the mind."[12] Any effort at all that an individual makes to deepen his or her understanding about the mind is said to dispel some of the darkness produced by the beliefs and habits that have collected there. "Just as a light within a pitcher does not shine outside, but when the latter is smashed the light will spread, so is it with our lives, a pitcher, and the radiant light, the lamp therein."[13] In this view, the closer one approaches the clear light of the mind, the greater the determination becomes to transform the whole world into a positive environment. At death, when all thought processes have ceased, the clear light of mind appears spontaneously in its full radiance and offers a once-in-a-lifetime, unobstructed, perfect chance to merge with it forever, just as easily as a child jumps into her mother's lap.[14] An individual who sees within his or her own deepest awareness even one glimmer of the clear light of mind—the source of all self-knowledge—has discovered a priceless buried treasure.[15]

Rebirth: The Realms of Cyclic Existence

> *This life will not be consumed without residue, like a candle, but we shall take other types of existence. Our situation is samsara, a continual round of rebirth.*[16]

In the Tibetan Buddhist view, when the body dies, the mind-continuum, the mind's most subtle essence of clear light,[17] separates from it and continues on into an afterdeath state and a future rebirth. The mind-continuum is swept along by the predispositions of thought and action that have been cultivated in it, lifetime after lifetime. Negative tendencies in the mind-continuum lead to habitual unhappiness and establish the causes for an unhappy rebirth, while positive tendencies cultivate joy and therefore lead to a happy rebirth. "As men think, so are they, both here and hereafter, thoughts being things, the parents of all actions, good and bad alike; and, as the sowing has been, so will the harvest be."[18]

In this view, because the predispositions of the mind are instrumental in determining the quality of a person's life—both now and in the future—it is important to purify the mind of negative habits and beliefs and to cultivate instead as many positive tendencies as possible. "This is my simple religion," says the Dalai Lama, "there is no need for temples; no need for complicated philosophy. Our own brain, our own heart is our temple; the philosophy is kindness."[19]

The Buddhist belief in rebirth is grounded in the teaching that no event or manifestation comes into being of its own accord. All events and manifestations are the result of previous causes. Any moment of mental activity, any act of consciousness, requires a preceding moment of mind or act of consciousness, which in turn requires another, and so on from beginningless time. All of the pasts, presents, and futures of an individual form an endless stream of continuity linked by the clear light of the mind-continuum, a mind state so subtle that it transcends not only the boundaries of the body but also the limits of time and space. Some enlightened individuals—masters and teachers such as the Dalai Lamas and Karmapas[20]—are highly aware of this continuity of the mind's essence and are so in tune with its rhythms that they leave clues for their followers that predict when and where they will reappear in a new incarnation.[21] Such individuals can also identify, as small children, certain objects that had belonged to them in their former lives. Tibetan Buddhists have encouraged Westerners to keep an open mind regarding rebirth, since to assume that it may be true carries no risk of harm, whereas to believe that it is not true limits understanding.[22]

Rebirth is said to occur in one of six realms of existence.[23] Three of the realms are considered to be woefully unhappy: the realm of hell beings, the realm of ghosts, and the realm of animals. Yet rebirth into one of them is said to be very possible as a direct result of the negative thoughts and actions that we are habitually carrying out right now. In fact, most of us are so strongly conditioned to react with at least some pessimism to our unfolding circumstances that negative habits can undermine even our most sincere efforts to develop positive tendencies. The three more fortunate realms are the human realm, the demigod realm, and the god realm. Rebirth into one of them is made possible by redirecting negative tendencies in the mind and cultivating goodness there instead.

Rebirth is not considered punishment or reward, no matter what realm a person is born into. A person is born into a particular realm as the direct result of the mental tendencies that prevail in his or her mind-continuum. An abundance of positive tendencies, for example, is the cause for being born into the god realm, a realm where the conditions are so favorable and produce such immediate and glorious happiness that the percipient dreads and fears change. As a result of such fears, selfish thoughts and actions arise and establish negative tendencies in the mind, and the positive forces responsible for the happy rebirth in the first place are slowly used up. Attachment to permanence and aversion to change produces negative tendencies in the mind-continuum in any realm. In the Tibetan tradition, the supreme benefit of being born into the human realm is that all humans have the ability to recognize and reduce the accumulation of negativity in the mind.

The Tibetan Book of the Dead:
An Instruction Manual

> *The knowledge of the path through the bardo must be gained "on this side" if it is to be put into practice "on the other side."*[24]

One treasure text that is familiar to many people in the West is *The Tibetan Book of the Dead*, first compiled and edited by W. Y. Evans-Wentz, based on a translation by Lama Kazi Dawa-Samdup. Drawn from a much larger collection of texts originally composed by Padmasambhava, one of the founders and most revered masters of Tibetan Buddhism, *The Tibetan Book of the Dead* has gone through a number of editions since the first in 1927. There have also been several new English translations of the original Padmasambhava manuscript.[25] As a result, the book is widely available in the United States.

Intended as much for the living as for the dying, *The Tibetan Book of the Dead* is a set of instructions designed to make plain and clear what happens during the transition from death to rebirth—a change that begins when the clear light of mind separates from the body at death and ends when the mind-continuum enters the womb of its next rebirth. After death, the mind-continuum enters the *bardo*, an unembodied interval between death and rebirth.[26] According to the tradition, the mind-continuum can stay in the bardo for as long as seven weeks, searching for an appropriate rebirth.[27] Each week in the bardo ends with a small death, and a new one begins upon awakening in the next phase of the after-death experience.

When the mind-continuum streams into the bardo it encounters the ordinary world transformed into a purified universe. With an illusory body (likened to the body we inhabit in a dream) the mind experiences "super-knowledge" and "perfect recall" and has awareness of spiritual teachings not necessarily known in the preceding life. In this state of mind, all objects and forms are "of the nature of rainbow light, completely clear and shining, vast and free of obstruction . . . transcending all limitations."[28]

During the first week in the bardo, peaceful deities inhabit the mind. These glorious and brilliant deities flow out of the heart energy of the perceiver as representatives of the most blissful and sublime of human emotions. If the mind at this time can recognize the panoramic array of peaceful deities as emanations from the heart center of the percipient, it will naturally merge with them. A mind in union with the deities is said to produce an ineffable sense of joy in the mind of the percipient, who will then view the world from a perspective that is totally free of coerced experience, completely happy in positive action, and fully empathetic with the environment. If by the end of the first week in the bardo the peaceful deities are not recognized, the percipient falls into a swoon and reawakens in the second week.[29]

During the second week in the bardo, the peaceful deities are transformed into their wrathful aspect. These wrathful deities do not exist in themselves but rather represent fully realized states emanating from the "brain-center" of the perceiver.[30] The wrathful deities are said to be extremely terrifying when they are not recognized as radiating from and created by one's own mind. As a consequence, fear can envelop the perceiver, who becomes overwhelmed and may try to escape. Now the chance to merge with the clear light is growing weaker. Yet the opportunity still remains to recognize any of the phenomena of the bardo as emanating from the mind of the perceiver—a realization that will trigger instant liberation into that same awareness, "brilliantly clear and radiant, transparent and multicolored, unlimited by any kind of dimension or direction, shimmering and constantly in motion."[31] Once liberated, the mind-continuum is no longer subject to the downward trajectory toward rebirth.

If the mind-continuum does not unite with the light during the panoramic display of the peaceful and wrathful deities, it persists in following the same habits and patterns established in the former life and continues to wander in the bardo searching for an appropriate rebirth. Soon the conventional world begins to materialize, and old favorite longings embedded within the mind come alive and draw it irresistibly into the realm of its next rebirth.[32]

The Tibetan Book of the Dead reminds the hearer that all experience is a reflection of the mind perceiving it, and that the ultimate power in realizing the omniscient potential of the mind is that it attracts one toward enlightenment. Whenever possible, Tibetan Buddhists leave the body of the deceased undisturbed for three to four days after death has occurred and read aloud from *The Tibetan Book of the Dead* in order to help the mind-continuum journey through the bardo. To give the flavor of the character of the instructions in *The Tibetan Book of the Dead*, I offer the following synthesis and adaptation of what might be read aloud in the first few days after death:

> Listen to me now, Margaret Coberly, you are dead. You have died and are now on the other side of this world. You are dead, and your old body has been left behind and a new one has not yet been found. This is the bardo state between death and re-birth. You are now in a mental realm. Listen to me. You are experiencing the radiance of the clear light, pure reality, the primordial ground of your mind. Recognize it, and do not be afraid. Because at death the energies and the elements of your body are reversed, many strange and frightening sensations are occurring, but this is a sign that you are in the bardo. Mountains, houses, and physical objects used to obstruct you, but now you can go anywhere you want simply by thinking about it. Everything is effortless. However, when you speak to friends and family there is no answer. All is twilight. No light comes from the sun, the moon, or the stars. The body that you have is entirely a reflection of your own mental ideas; it has no substance, it casts no shadow. These are the signs of the bardo. Look into your mind and recognize that whatever appears is the reflection of your own consciousness; even what is terrifying is but the reflection of your own perception. Therefore, do not be afraid, do not be angry, but exercise your compassion and love.[33]

In the early 1980s, the Dalai Lama spoke about using *The Tibetan Book of the Dead* as a practical tool in the West. "In general," he said, "without the preparation of initiation, meditation, and so forth, this would be difficult. It is necessary to be familiar with the teachings."[34] However, Robert Thurman, the popular writer and scholar at Columbia University, has published a translation of *The Tibetan Book of the Dead* intended to make the readings more accessible to Westerners. Thurman writes in the preface that he specifically set out to "produce a version that would be simple and useful, easy for bereaved relatives to read, and easy for lost souls to hear in the room where they anxiously hover about their corpses and wonder what has happened to them."[35]

The Tibetan Book of the Dead can be a valuable resource for caregivers even if it is not used directly in caring for the dying. Filled with gemlike insights about the nature of the human mind, it has value on many different levels. Overall, it challenges and encourages us to see death as a process, a transition, and a spiritual journey. Adopting this kind of attitude toward death can greatly assist caregivers in creating a peaceful and positive environment for the dying.

5

The Eight Stages
of Dissolution

We, like parted drops of rain,
Swelling till they meet and run,
Shall be all absorbed again,
Melting, flowing into one.

—CHRISTOPHER CRANCH,
Gnosis

AS A PROFESSIONAL CAREGIVER, I HAVE
found that my search for effective ways to interact
with people who are dying has been significantly illuminated by
the many wise and practical instructions that permeate the Tibetan Buddhist literature on death and dying. But the most en-
riching and psychologically helpful Tibetan Buddhist teaching
about death and dying, for me, is the description of the eight dissolutions leading to death. The precise nature of these teachings
provide an easy-to-read map through the unknown territory of

dying, and can easily be used by Westerners who may want to broaden their understanding about the dying trajectory.

According to Tibetan Buddhism, the dying process begins when the body is first afflicted with a terminal illness and ends when the mind-continuum exits the body. As a person dies, eight stages of dissolution take place. These stages of dissolution relate to five elements—earth, water, fire, wind, and space—and to five aggregates of individuality: forms, feelings, discriminations, compositional factors, and ordinary consciousness. Each of the elements and aggregates is said to have a specific representation in the body.[1]

When the elements that compose the body dissolve, ordinary consciousness is absorbed back into its most subtle and natural state—clear light—and then exits the body. The Tibetan tradition describes in detail the external and internal signs that are produced as each stage of dissolution takes place.[2] Throughout the aging process, for example, signs that the earth element is slowly dissolving can be seen as the skin wrinkles, the bones weaken, and the body shrinks. The other dissolutions are less obvious and seem to occur very close to the time of actual death, yet each does have accompanying signs that can often be directly observed during a dying trajectory. Should a person have the misfortune to die in a violent accident or sudden death, the dissolutions and their signs are said to occur as quickly as a flash.[3]

In the West, a person is pronounced dead when the vital signs—respiration, blood pressure, and pulse—cease. In the Tibetan tradition, however, the cessation of the vital signs is a signal not of death but rather of the dissolution of wind into space, the fourth of the eight stages. In this view, after a person stops breathing four more stages of dissolution remain before he or she is considered dead.

The concept of the eight stages of dissolution leading to death has existed for centuries in Tibet, providing a practical and familiar framework for understanding what happens during dying. In the West, we have no such map for people traveling through the

The Five Elements

Element	Representation in the Body	Aggregate of Individuality	Associated Sense
Earth	Bones, muscles, skin, nails	*Forms:* things that constitute the physical world	Vision: colors and shapes
Water	Blood, lymph, secretions	*Feelings:* sensations associated with forms	Hearing: sounds
Fire	Body temperature	*Discriminations:* differentiations based on feelings	Smell: odors
Wind	Respirations	*Compositional factors:* good and bad volitional activities	Taste: tastes Touch: touches
Space	Body orifices and channels	*Ordinary consciousness:* eighty thought states	Ordinary thoughts

unknown territory of dying. The lack of information and fear that has been generated by our cultural inclination to deny death can be reduced by an open-minded study of the Tibetan Buddhist teachings about death. The theory of the dissolution of the elements provides a workable strategy for charting the course of a dying trajectory. It can be used as a guide and as such can eliminate some of the confusion that arises from not knowing what will happen next.

While caring for people who are dying, I have often observed that certain predictable physical patterns unfold, especially as death's approach gathers speed. When I first read about the Tibetan Buddhist stages of dissolution, I was immediately struck by how well they matched my own observations. I began to use this revealing road map more generally as a way to chart a course through the unknown terrain of a person's dying trajectory. In the following discussion of each dissolution and its signs, I offer some practical applications and suggestions for care providers.[4] (This information is summarized in a chart on pages 94–98.)

Stage 1: Earth Dissolves into Water (Mirage)

The first cycle in the eight stages of dissolution leading to death begins when the earth element dissolves into, and is absorbed by, the water element, causing the more solid components of the body, the parts associated with the earth element, such as bones, flesh, teeth, hair, and nails, to deteriorate and lose their ability to function.[5] The hair thins, teeth become fragile, and limbs dwindle. The mind-continuum is now beginning its separation from the body. At this time the dying person is said to experience a feeling of powerlessness and a sense of deep heaviness that feels like sinking.

I have often heard dying people complain about an overwhelming exhaustion and weakness that overtakes them as death approaches, a fatigue so powerful that it renders them dependent on others for help with even the most minor of tasks. As the body continues to deteriorate and the muscles weaken and fail, even the ability to hold up one's head may be lost. The strong sinking sensation that accompanies the dissolution of the earth element can cause dying people to call out, "Pull me up," or "I'm falling, hold me up," or "Lift me up, I'm sinking." Some dying people may ask the caregiver to remove even the lightest of blankets because they feel too heavy.

About three weeks before my brother died, I was sitting on the landing of the stairwell that led down into his bedroom, a perch that afforded an almost full view of the room below. Wheeler looked very small and far away lying in his huge bed, even though he was no more than fifteen feet away. His head was propped up with pillows on both sides. His body slumped into the blankets that had been firmly tucked under his thighs. He looked up at me and said, "You look so far away. I wish that I could come up there, that you could lift me up out of whatever I am sinking into. It feels like something heavy is pushing me into the ground." At the time, I had no explanation for what he was experiencing and didn't know what I could do to make him more comfortable, either physically or psychologically.

People who have knowledge about the stages of dissolution can anticipate some of the needs that a person may develop as the dying process unfolds. The feeling of heaviness and the sense of sinking that results from the earth element dissolving, for example, can be relieved on the physical level by simple measures such as keeping the dying person's head elevated, and by using a footboard to keep blankets lifted off the feet and lower extremities. An interesting phenomenon that seems to happen at this stage is that the dying person's internal sense of extreme heaviness often translates into his or her body actually feeling heavier to those providing the care, and additional help is required just to move the person in the bed. One way to help reduce the sense of heaviness that is bearing down on a dying person is to try to minimize the negative input of emotionalism and anxiety that may be contributed by family, friends, or other care providers who are themselves afraid of death and unable to be at peace.

As a dying person's eye muscles lose strength, the eyes may not open or close completely, or they may roll uncontrollably to one side or the other or upward into the head. It is a natural reaction to try and rouse a person whose eyes are rolled back and fixed open, but when someone is dying, it is more appropriate to just place a cool moist pad over the eyes and lower the window shades to diffuse the light.

During the dissolution of the earth element, vision dims and the ability to perceive and distinguish shapes decreases. The dissolving mind-body connection produces much mental turmoil that can result in the dying person having angry emotional outbursts. As the mental state grows increasingly confused, some dying people have difficulty remembering the present physical condition of illness and describe being overcome by a feeling that they are the "victim of an intrigue."[6] At times, a dying person has whispered to me in confidence, "Someone is trying to kill me," or "Someone is poisoning my food." These moments of confusion will require special reassurances for the dying person as well as for the others in attendance. To help allay the bewilderment that a dying person can experience at this point, speak clearly and directly, and avoid unnecessary conversation around the bedside.

The Tibetan Buddhist teachings do not offer clear guidelines about the time required for each stage of dissolution. Signs of the earth element beginning to dissolve are often clearly visible in old people even if they are not otherwise terminally ill: their bones become frail, their teeth fall out, and their eyesight fails. In my experience, during some dying trajectories signs of the earth element dissolving can last for as long as several weeks or more. When the earth element completes its dissolution into the water element, the mind is said to fill with the appearance of a silver-blue mirage—likened to the illusion of water vaporizing on a scorching highway.

Stage 2: Water Dissolves into Fire (Smoke)

During the second of the eight stages of dissolution, the water element is absorbed by the fire element. Initially the water element swells because the earth element has dissolved into it, and this is said to cause the dying person to experience a sensation of drowning or being swept away by torrents of water. This feeling is soon replaced, however, by one of intense dehydration, as the water element is absorbed into fire, and the liquids of the body such as lymph, blood, urine, sweat, saliva, tears, and phlegm dry up. External signs include a feeling of heat and parchedness that causes the dying person's mouth and throat to become extremely dry and scum to form on the teeth; then an overwhelming feeling of thirst ensues, and the person may call out for water.

As the water element dissolves, feelings of pleasure and pain fade. Now the dying person is less able to pay attention to what is happening, and he or she may no longer feel much physical pain. In my experience, sometimes a dying person will suddenly deny having any physical pain at all and refuse any further pain medication. In the past, on these occasions I often would give the routine pain medication anyway, because at the time it was impossible for me to believe that a dying person could suddenly stop feeling pain. "She must not know what she is feeling," I would think, or "He must be hallucinating."

In the Tibetan Buddhist view, a person is likely not to experience any further physical pain when the water element is absorbed into fire, because the aggregate of feeling is also fading at this time. In the case of a person who denies having discomfort and who asks not to be medicated for pain, it is okay to omit the pain medication not only because the patient doesn't want it, but also because pain medication has a strong tendency to dull the mind, especially when it is not required.[7]

Care providers who are aware of the sequence of events that occur during the dissolution of the elements can anticipate during this stage that the dying person will have diminished body fluids and difficulty swallowing. Ice chips made of frozen juice or water or a wet cloth to suck on may be all that the dying person can tolerate at this point. A damp cloth behind the neck or on the forehead can also help to relieve the intense feeling of heat and dehydration.

As the dying person loses interest in worldly affairs and is no longer able to pay attention to external circumstances, he or she may completely withdraw from friends and relatives, who then feel rejected and upset by the sudden change. An informed care provider can be especially supportive at this time by helping friends and relatives to understand that the dying person's withdrawal is not a turn *away* from them, but rather a natural turn *inward*. Now the mind-body connection is growing even weaker, and it is increasingly important to protect the dying person's mind from confusion and fright. Upset loved ones should try to refrain from disrupting the peace.

The internal sign said to arise in the mind as the water element is absorbed into fire is the appearance of billowing puffs of white smoke, similar to the smoke that rises from a chimney.

Stage 3: Fire Dissolves into Wind (Fireflies)

The third stage of dissolution occurs when the fire element is absorbed into the wind. Now the components of the body that represent fire, those related to the production of the body's inner heat, such as the hypothalamus and the thyroid, malfunction and fade. At this stage, a dying person may initially suffer from a sense of being consumed by fire, but then later feel very cold as the wind element increases. The ability to digest food diminishes and eventually is lost altogether. Respiration changes too; inhalations become short and weak, while exhalations are drawn out and strong. The upper and lower extremities begin to mottle. As the warmth of the body moves from the extremities toward the torso, the dying person may require extra socks or leggings. At this stage, oxygen or a fan can be of great help to the dying person to reduce the sense of breathlessness caused by faltering respirations.

As fire is absorbed into wind, the ability to discriminate fades and the mind becomes progressively more unfocused and inattentive to external activities and unable to discriminate between people, objects, and words. I have been with dying people who, all of a sudden, do not recognize family members anymore and even become extremely disturbed or frightened when they see them standing at the bedside. Understandably, this can be very upsetting to the loved ones, and informed care providers can offer some reassurance simply by explaining that the dying person's mind is no longer able to follow what is happening around him or her.

Because the mind-body connection is now so weak, ordinary consciousness is very dim and it is especially important to avoid disturbing the dying person's mind. In the Tibetan Buddhist view, protecting the mind from agitation will predispose it to the positive mental tendencies established by former virtuous actions. A positive mental outlook at the time of death is especially important because, as the Dalai Lama says, it will "provide the impetus for lifetimes in happy migrations."[8]

The internal sign said to appear in the mind as the fire element dissolves into wind is one of tiny red dots of light, like fireflies, or the sparks that dance in the smoke of an outdoor flame.

Stage 4: Wind Dissolves into Space (Flame)

As the wind element is absorbed into space, the dying person's respirations become increasingly shallow and may begin to rattle (this is what is known as the "death rattle" in Western medicine), and a thickening and darkening of the tongue is said to occur.[9] Soon the sporadic respirations produce longer and longer pauses between exhalation and inhalation, the rattling becomes less and less frequent, and then there is silence: the pulse fades to nothing, the heart has stopped. The silence that follows is so deafening that it usually shocks those who are present. In Western medicine this is the official moment of death, a time when much activity and upset starts to occur around the dying person. Some people become hysterical, while others busy themselves with frantic activity around the bedside.

Within the Tibetan Buddhist framework, after the heart stops beating, four more stages of dissolution remain before the mind-continuum completes its separation from the body. Therefore, it is now extremely important to protect the concentration of the dying person's mind, and not distract it with the sorrows of those who are left behind. By keeping a light touch on the dying person's pulse a care provider can monitor the deteriorating physical condition, and at the same time encourage and prepare family members and other loved ones to remain calm and strong for the sake of the person who is dying.[10]

As the wind element dissolves into space, ordinary consciousness of worldly purposes and activities fades, and the person is no longer aware of external forces. Many different experiences and visions are said to now arise in the dying person's mind, in accord with the mental tendencies that prevail there. For example, people who are impelled by negativity, anger, and violence will see the "Lord of Death"—a terrifying personification of their own powerlessness over death. Others who have strong positive tendencies may experience deities and angels arriving to take them to another existence. During and after the death of a Tibetan Buddhist, portions of *The Tibetan Book of the Dead* are read out loud to guide the dying and explain what is happening. For Westerners, it can help to speak softly and talk to the dying person, urging him or her to move onward, to leave the body and merge with the peace, happiness, and light that is beckoning.

The internal sign said to arise in the mind as the wind element is absorbed into space is like the appearance of a sputtering flame in a dark room, or a flame that is about to go out.

Stage 5: Ordinary Mind States Dissolve (White Flash)

During the fifth stage, it is said that the eighty thought states of the ordinary mind dissolve. These thought states are categorized into three groups according to the amount of tenacity and firmness with which they are held. The first group consists of thirty-three states of mind that are considered to be the most tenacious and unwavering, such as various levels of sorrow, fear, attachment, nonvirtue, hunger, thirst, and feeling. In the second group are thought states said to be less compelling than those in the first, such as rapture, effort, pride, vehemence, heroism, and deceit. The third group contains the least powerful thought states called the seven delusions—not wanting to speak, doubt, forgetfulness, mistakenness, laziness, depression, and ambiguity.

All of the ordinary mind states are absorbed into a more basic and subtle consciousness called the mind of radiant white appearance. As the conceptualizations in the mind disappear, the internal vision is said to change from a sputtering flame to a steady flame.

Through an intricate and complex system of physiological channels and winds described in Tibetan tradition, the dissolution of the eighty thought states causes the psychophysiological masculine principle in the form of a white drop[11] to descend from the crown of the head and move downward toward the heart—a movement that produces a radiant white appearance in the mind, said to be like a vivid black night sky that is "flooded in moonlight."[12] Although adepts are able to sustain the radiant white appearance in the mind by recognizing it and merging with it, ordinary people experience it only as an instantaneous white flash.[13]

Stages 6–8: Subtle Mind States Dissolve (Red Flash, Black Flash, Clear Light)

The last three stages of the dissolutions leading to death involve the mind dissolving into its most subtle forms. Ordinary people are said to experience these last stages as rapid and brief flashes. In stage six the mind of radiant white appearance dissolves into an even more subtle mind state known as the mind of "radiant red increase" and causes the psychophysiological female principle, in the form of a red drop, to ascend from the base of the spine and move upward toward the heart—a movement that produces the appearance of a "clear vacuity filled with red light."[14] In the seventh stage, the mind of radiant red increase dissolves into the mind of "black near-attainment" ("near-attainment" because the mind of clear light will soon appear) and causes the descending white drop that represents the male principle and the ascending red drop that represents the female principle to meet in the heart. When the red and white drops meet, they envelop between them the indestructible drop that is said to reside in the center of the heart. The indestructible drop represents the most refined and subtle essence of the mind, and when it becomes surrounded in this way by the white and red drops, an appearance of vivid blackness is produced in the mind.

In the last stage, the mind of black near-attainment dissolves into the indestructible drop at the center of the heart, and the clear light of death dawns. Said to be brighter than the brightest sun magnified a thousand times, the pristine luminosity of the mind of clear light at death appears to even the tiniest insect. In one instant the mind rests completely in its own true nature. At this moment many beings are said to attain liberation from the cycle of rebirth by recognizing the clear light of death as the essence of their own mind, the original source of all experience. By recognizing it, they are not afraid and thus they are able to remain in blissful union with it. The clear light is said to persist for three to four days before the mind-continuum exits the body. However, most individuals are so overcome when they first encounter the radiance of the clear light that they fall into a swoon for the entire time and awaken to find themselves in the bardo.[15]

Tibetan Buddhists leave the body undisturbed for three or four days after respirations have ceased, to allow the mind-continuum to remain in the clear light of death as long as possible prior to its exit from the body. It is said that violent handling of the body "can only disturb the end processes of death, possibly resulting in a lower rebirth."[16] Care providers or loved ones may find the idea of allowing a dead body to remain undisturbed for more than a few hours repugnant, since in the West it is considered unhealthy and unsanitary. The idea of deliberately leaving a dead body in plain view for very long is psychologically abhorrent to Western medical personnel, so in hospitals dead people are immediately removed from sight.

Since it is usually not possible to leave a dead body alone for more than several hours, even at home, one way to reduce the amount of jostling and touching that the deceased undergoes while being moved from the bed and transported to the mortuary is to prearrange for a simple transport box. After a ceremony of cleaning and dressing the body, or whatever ritual the loved ones wish to perform, gently place the body into the box where it can remain throughout transport and for three days (if appropriate and desired) until cremation or burial. If the dying person and the family want such arrangements, they can be made ahead of time with the mortuary.

The definitive signs that indicate departure of the mind-continuum from the body are said to be a white or red drop appearing as blood or puslike white fluid at the nostril, in the mouth, or at the tip of the urethra. According to Tibetan tradition, these external signs will not appear in a body that has been ravaged by illness.[17] In any case, the body will start to decompose or smell bad once the mind-continuum has departed from it.

There are reports about realized beings who have remained in extraordinary states for many days after vital signs have ceased. Two Tibetan Buddhist lamas who died in American hospitals are examples. They demonstrated to Western medical personnel and many others who were in attendance the resourcefulness and depth of the Tibetan Buddhist view of death and dying and the principles described in the eight stages of dissolution leading to death.

The Tibetan Art of Death: Two Lamas

Rangjung Rigpe Dorje, the sixteenth Gyalwa Karmapa,[18] first visited the United States during the 1970s. He traveled extensively, teaching Tibetan Buddhist practices to many thousands of people. In 1981, the Karmapa returned to the United States, this time under very different circumstances. He had had surgery for stomach cancer and was seeking follow-up treatment with an American physician. He was admitted to the American International Hospital in Zion, Illinois, where he later died. His physician, Dr. Mitchell Levy, said that the Karmapa's "overflowing, unceasing kindness" overwhelmed the staff who were "constantly confronted with this patient who was dying, but who was still more concerned about them . . . than he was about himself."[19]

The Karmapa made many friends in the hospital even while close to death, and was so respected by the Western medical personnel there that they allowed his body to remain in the hospital bed unmoved for the customary three days after vital signs had ceased. According to Dr. Levy, during those postmortem days the Karmapa's body showed no signs of decay, nor did it omit any unpleasant odors, a fact that astonished the medical community. Even more surprising, especially to the physicians, was that seventy-two hours after his respirations had ceased, hospital documentation showed that the Karmapa's body was still warm over the heart area. Dr. Levy said that as a physician he had no explanation for this.[20] According to Tibetan Buddhist theory, the continued warmth over the heart would be produced during the seventh stage of dissolution, when the red and white drops meet and surround the indestructible drop at the center of the heart.

Another lama who died in an American hospital and demonstrated to others the principles of the stages of dissolution leading to death was Lama Thubten Yeshe. Lama Yeshe became a powerful influence in the lives of thousands of Westerners through his extensive teaching and writing.[21] Lama Yeshe had chronic rheumatic heart disease and in 1974 was given a terminal diagnosis by a group of physicians in Wisconsin. He said, "What they don't see is that the human being is something special. We are beyond the ordinary concept of what people think we are."[22] The lama lived for ten more years, traveling and spreading Buddhist wisdom throughout the world, before he returned to California to die in the care of his students. When Lama Yeshe's condition worsened gravely, he was taken to Cedars-Sinai Medical Center in Los Angeles, where, at the age of forty-nine, he eventually died in the coronary care unit.

A nurse there reported that he was laughing, joking, and "embracing us up to the split second when his heart stopped. . . . In this way, he showed us that death was ordinary, nothing to be afraid about."[23] These words are particularly touching in light of what Lama Yeshe had written to a friend earlier about the way his mind had become filled with pain and confusion while in the hospital: "Due to powerful medicines, unending injections and oxygen tubes just to breathe . . . I realized that it is extremely difficult to maintain awareness . . . during the stages of death."[24] After Lama Yeshe was pronounced dead, the administrative personnel at the hospital were unwilling to allow his body to remain in the room undisturbed for the customary three-day postmortem period, but they did allow his body to be moved to and remain in a little-used area of the hospital. Here, many prayers were conducted and traditional Tibetan Buddhist prostrations carried out. People who viewed the body over the three days after the vital signs had stopped said that it was a beautiful golden color and never showed any signs of decay.[25]

Tibetan Buddhist teachings offer a new approach to understanding death and dying, one that can be implemented in the West by both professional and lay care providers. The chart that follows summarizes the dissolution of the elements leading to death and the internal and external signs that are said to appear along with practical suggestions for providing care at each stage.

SUMMARY TABLE OF THE EIGHT STAGES OF DISSOLUTION

Factor Dissolving	External Signs	Internal Signs	Suggestions for Care Providers
1. EARTH			
Solid parts of the body, such as the bones, teeth, and nails	The body weakens and feels heavy; the neck can't support the head. Complaints of sinking and feeling weighted down by the bedcovers.	The mind is confused and prone to emotional outbursts, depression, and paranoia.	▪ Keep the head elevated on pillows. ▪ Use a footboard to lift bedcovers off the legs. ▪ Obtain help to turn or lift the dying person.
Vision	Difficulty opening or closing the eyes; the eyes roll up into the head.	The mental image or internal appearance that appears is like a silver-blue *mirage*.	▪ Be aware of sensitivity to light. Use moist cloths or pads to cover the eyes; lower the window shades.
The aggregate of individuality that perceives form	Vision dims and the physical world becomes unclear.		▪ Keep overly emotional friends calm and undisruptive.
2. WATER			
Liquid elements of the body such as blood, lymph, tears, phlegm, urine, saliva, sweat, and semen	Bodily fluids dry up; fever and dryness; scum forms on the teeth; sweating followed by a feeling of coldness.	The mind becomes hazy, nervous, and irritable.	▪ Provide mouth swabs, ice chips, cold bland juice, or wet cloth to suck on. ▪ Maintain a calm, serene atmosphere.
Hearing	Hearing loss.	The mental image or internal appearance is of white puffs of smoke billowing from a chimney or blue-gray *smoke* in the room.	▪ Let visitors and loved ones know that emotional withdrawal is expected and a normal part of the dying trajectory.
The aggregate of individuality that experiences feeling	No more feelings of pain or pleasure; indifference.		

3. FIRE

Inner heat and metabolism: hypothalamus and thyroid	The warmth of the body fades and the extremities mottle.	The mind is alternately clear and unclear, hardly recognizing anything.	■ Be prepared for temperature fluctuations.
Smell	Smell diminishes, digestion fails, and respirations become difficult with short inhalations and long exhalations.	The mental image that appears is sparks of light occurring in the smoke, similar to sparks over an outdoor flame or *fireflies*.	■ Have a fan available to let fresh air into the room if appropriate. ■ Have oxygen available. ■ Reassure the dying person that it is okay to let go.
The aggregate of individuality responsible for discrimination	No longer mindful of loved ones' names or daily affairs.		■ Support family members as dying person withdraws even more.

4. WIND

Respiration and winds in the body	The breath rattles with long exhalations and short and difficult inhalations; eye movements slow down.	Visions arise according to the person's tendencies—those impelled by negativity may see the "Lord of Death" and be terrified; those impelled by positive tendencies may see deities or angels.	■ Keep the room free of turmoil and allow the dying person to have peaceful last thoughts.
Taste	Taste fails, tongue thickens, sense faculties completely cease. Breathing stops.	The mental vision or image is like that of a *sputtering flame*.	■ Encourage loved ones to remain calm and focused on feelings of love and gratitude for the life of the dying person.
The aggregate of individuality made up of compositional factors that motivate action or volition	The dying person is no longer aware of the external world.		■ Try not to jostle or handle the deceased roughly, since the more subtle levels of mind have yet to dissolve before the mind-continuum separates from the body.

Summary Table of the Eight Stages of Dissolution (continued)

Factor Dissolving	External Signs	Internal Signs	Suggestions for Care Providers
5. EIGHTY CONCEPTIONS: ORDINARY MIND			
The thirty-three thought states associated with greatest involvement such as different levels of sorrow, fear, attachment, nonvirtue, hunger, thirst, and feeling	Not specified.	As the eighty thought states dissolve the internal vision that appears is like a red *steady flame*.	■ Since all eight stages of dissolution are said to occur whether a person is aware of them or not, it may help the dying person if the caregiver and loved ones remember that these dissolutions continue even after breathing has ceased.
The forty more subtle thought states such as rapture, effort, pride, vehemence, heroism, and deceit		After the eighty concepts dissolve, the white drop at the top of the head moves downward toward the heart, and the subtle mind of radiant white appearance dawns. The internal vision is of a *radiant white sky*, similar to a night sky filled with moonlight.	■ Only allow the body to be handled very gently during the ritual of cleaning and dressing that often occurs after breathing has ceased; then let the body remain undisturbed for a period of time that is appropriate to the individual circumstances.
The seven deluded thought states of not wanting to speak, doubt, forgetfulness, mistakenness, laziness, depression, and ambiguity			

6. MIND OF RADIANT WHITE APPEARANCE

The subtle mind of radiant white appearance dissolves into the even more subtle mind of radiant red increase.

Not specified.

Dissolution of the subtle mind of radiant white appearance causes the red drop at the base of the spine to move upward toward the heart.

The internal vision is a *radiant red sky* similar to a clear sky pervaded by sunlight.

The subtle mind of radiant white appearance may only be seen as a brief white flash in the mind of the dying person, and the mind of radiant red increase may only be seen as a brief red flash (the length of time the dying person sees the lights of the subtle minds is said to depend on the dying person's spiritual awareness).

- Remember that the dying process continues even though the person is no longer breathing. To help the dying through the remaining stages of dissolution it's beneficial to maintain an atmosphere of serenity and calm. Keep the loved ones involved in positive activities that promote that kind of environment such as singing, praying, or helping the other bereaved.

Factor Dissolving	External Signs	Internal Signs	Suggestions for Care Providers
7. MIND OF RADIANT RED INCREASE			
The more subtle mind of radiant red increase dissolves into the even more subtle mind of radiant black near-attainment.	Not specified.	Dissolution of the mind of radiant red increase causes the ascending red drop and the descending white drop to meet and envelop the indestructible drop in the heart. The internal vision is the appearance of a *radiant black sky*, followed by a swoon.	▪ Avoid having the body handled roughly by strangers from the morgue or funeral home. For transport to the morgue, a simple pine box can be purchased ahead of time, and the body gently placed in it, after cleaning rituals are completed.
8. MIND OF BLACK NEAR-ATTAINMENT			
The subtle mind of black near-attainment dissolves into the most subtle mind, the clear light of mind.	As long as one recognizes the clear light of mind and remains united with it, the body does not decompose. A white or red drop (such as puss or blood) may appear at the nostril, in the mouth, or at the tip of the urethra.	Dissolution of the red and white drops into the indestructible drop at the heart releases the most subtle essence of the mind into the clear light. The moment of death is marked by the appearance of luminous, primordial *clear light*, said to appear even to the tiniest insect.	▪ The clear light manifests for three to four days, whether one falls into a swoon or not. After that time the mind-continuum (in most cases) separates from the body altogether. If the family wishes to be certain that the mind-continuum has departed the body prior to burial or cremation, arrange with the mortuary to postpone the final disposal for three to four days.

PART THREE

PRACTICAL APPLICATIONS FOR CARE PROVIDERS

Like as the waves make towards the pebbled shore,
So do our minutes hasten to their end;
Each changing place with that which goes before,
In sequent toil all forwards do contend.

WILLIAM SHAKESPEARE, Sonnet LX

6

Tibetan Buddhist Practice and the Dying Trajectory

> *Fear no more the frown o' the great,*
> *Thou art past the tyrant's stroke;*
> *Care no more to clothe and eat;*
> *To thee the reed is as the oak:*
> *The sceptre, learning, physic, must*
> *All follow this, and come to dust.*
>
> —WILLIAM SHAKESPEARE,
> *Cymbeline*

DURING THE LAST HALF OF THE TWENTI-
eth century, the "art of dying"—*artes moriendi,*[1] experienced a revival in the United States. The idea of death with
dignity found expression and began to flourish in the hospice
movement's palliative model of care.[2] Focused on healing rather
than curing, palliative care has evolved into a specialty that includes many different adjuncts to traditional medicine, such as
meditation, visualization, and prayer. But at the most fundamental level there is still a gap between an external, intellectual

knowing about death and dying and an internal experiential *realization* about impermanence and the certainty of death.

In the East the cultivation of a realistic view about the inevitability of change and the inescapability of death is regarded as very important. In Tibetan Buddhist psychology, a lack of death awareness is considered to be the door to all troubles, because failure to cultivate an awareness of death allows worldly desire to grow without restraint and virtuous action to be postponed. It is said that if a person doesn't remember the possibility of death first thing in the morning, the entire day will be spent in the pursuit of self-centered, short-term gains and the welfare of others will be of little concern. To consider the welfare of others is important in the Tibetan Buddhist view because kind and generous motives transform negative forces in the mind, and when a person replaces negative tendencies with positive ones, suffering is diminished both now and in the future. To act in a way that eases suffering—not just superficially and temporarily, but perfectly and forever—is a fundamental requirement for happiness according to this tradition. The Buddha said, "Our own intentions are the best way to be kind to ourselves."[3] Generous intentions toward others can diminish suffering for anyone, even people who are "brutal and intent on their own aims."[4] It is easy to directly observe the effects of having good intentions or bad ones: for example, how the momentary happiness that is caused by vain goals and self-centered concerns often turns to disappointment and becomes a source of long-term dissatisfaction. In the words of the Dalai Lama, "The more selfish and self-centered you remain, the more lonely and miserable you become."[5]

Tibetan Buddhism posits that an altruistic motivation is likely to arise naturally in people who realize that the problems and miseries associated with birth, aging, sickness, and death are shared universally and equally by people everywhere. No person wants to suffer, yet ironically, all people must endure the greatest suffering there is—death. To realize and reflect on the truth of death and how all of us are equal at the moment of death can weaken boundaries and foster compassion. The Tibetan Buddhist death meditation nurtures a compassionate point of view by reminding a person that death, in the end, will level even the greatest king. The meditation is a simple but profound technique to begin facing death, even for those Westerners who have had little or no exposure to death and dying.

The Tibetan Buddhist Death Meditation

Tibetan Buddhism advocates daily reflection on death not for the purpose of generating anxiety or sadness, but for making death more familiar now so that it won't be such a shock later. In this view, training the mind to remember the inevitability and unpredictability of death helps to both increase awareness of the present and erode illusions about the future. Like much of Tibetan Buddhist doctrine, the death meditation is laid out in a precise and exacting manner. The three root ideas of the meditation are (1) death is certain, (2) the time of death is uncertain, and (3) at the time of death nothing is of value except the condition of the mind. Each root idea has three specific reasons to support it, and each ends with a resolution.

1. Death is certain.
   No one can elude death.
   Any life diminishes without interruption.
   There is little time for spiritual practice and improving mental tendencies.

   RESOLUTION: Since death is certain, I resolve to practice spiritual teachings to improve and transform the condition of my mind.

2. The time of death is uncertain.
   The life span of a human being is very uncertain.
   Many circumstances lead to death.
   The body is weak and susceptible to harm.

RESOLUTION: I resolve to practice spiritual teachings and transform the condition of my mind, now, while there is still time.

3. At the time of death nothing is of value except the condition of the mind.
   Friends and relatives cannot accompany a person at death.
   No material possessions can accompany a person at death.
   The body is of no further use after death.

   RESOLUTION: I resolve to practice spiritual teachings and transform the condition of my mind, now, while there is still time, without further procrastination.

A person examines the first root idea—*Death is certain*—by evaluating the three reasons why death is certain. The first reason is that no one has ever escaped death. People have tried in different ways to outdistance death, but no one has ever succeeded. "Even the learned scholar cannot postpone it with his eloquence," Milarepa said. "No coward like a fox can sneak away."[6] The second reason death is certain is that every life has a definite limit and each day that passes brings it closer. Life is brief. The third reason death is certain is that people don't cultivate the positive mental tendencies that would, according to this tradition, eventually lead to liberation from the cycles of death and rebirth. When a person realizes that death is certain and that the condition of the mind is all that is of value at the time of death, a resolution naturally arises to transform the condition of the mind by cultivating positive tendencies in it.

A person examines the second root idea—*The time of death is uncertain*—by contemplating the truth of its three reasons. The first reason is that the life span of a human being is uncertain: some people awaken in the morning and are dead that night; some people die very young, some die very old. Death can happen at any time. The second reason the time of death is uncertain is that there are many circumstances that lead to death. For example, hundreds of people die every day as the result of internal physiological imbalances such as disease, poison, wrong medicine, rotten food, and autoimmune conditions. Hundreds also die from external conditions: of the more than two million deaths in the United States last year, over twenty thousand of them were the result of murders and another forty-three thousand were caused by automobile accidents.[7] The third reason the time of death is uncertain is that even though the body appears permanent and substantial, it is actually fragile and quite susceptible to disease and other adverse conditions. When a person realizes that the time of death is uncertain and that there are many causes that can bring it about at any time, a resolution naturally arises to transform the condition of the mind now. Since, at death, all that will remain of value are the mental tendencies that have been cultivated in the mind, individuals determine their own future both now and in the next lifetime. The Buddha said as he died, "All things are impermanent. Work out your own salvation with diligence."[8]

A person examines the third root idea of the death meditation—*At the time of death nothing is of value except the condition of the mind*—by contemplating what there is of value at the time of death. First, there are no friends that accompany a person at death. Second, there are no possessions that a person can keep at death. And third, even one's own body must remain behind at death. At death, all a person has to rely on is his or her own mind and the mental tendencies that have been conditioned there— tendencies that determine the quality of the next life. When a person remembers that nothing more is of value at the time of death except the condition of the mind, the resolution naturally arises to transform its condition now, while there is still time. By restraining self-centered tendencies and nurturing positive concerns now, a person won't be overwhelmed with regret, at death, for not having developed the positive tendencies that determine a happy rebirth and lead to liberation from the cycles of existence.

Kalu Rinpoche tells us that human beings are "pivotally poised" between two possibilities: endless wandering in *samsara* (cyclic rebirth) as a result of self-centered motives or transcending samsara as a result of concern for the welfare of others. He writes, "Both possibilities stem from the mind that each and every one of us has and experiences."[9]

To contemplate death often and systematically, as in the Tibetan Buddhist death meditation, can help people become more familiar with the inevitability of death and less afraid of it when it actually arrives. In this way, the terror that arises at hearing a terminal diagnosis can be diminished, both for the person who is ill and for his or her loved ones.

Hearing the Diagnosis: Death Is Certain

The first time I heard a formal "terminal diagnosis" was when my friend Michael became ill. We were both twenty-two years old at the time, and I was in nursing school. Michael had asked me to go with him to the lung surgeon's office to hear the results of some tests that had been taken to diagnose a chronic cough he had developed. We were both a little nervous as we waited in the physician's office, but I hadn't even considered the possibility that there might be something seriously wrong. The physician seemed so powerful and trustworthy to me as he swept into the room and slid several X rays into the view box on the wall behind his desk. With a brief glance and a nod at Michael, he turned to the films and slowly traced his finger around a very irregular, ominous-looking shadow. "Michael," he said, "I am sorry, but we have to consider this malignant until proven otherwise." His words were like a bomb that exploded the myth I had of a guaranteed future. It had to be a mistake. "People our age don't die," I thought, as my panic mounted. The illusion of fixed circumstances was slipping from my grip and I wanted to get away fast. When Michael looked at me for reassurance, I couldn't think of anything to say. Once we got out of the physician's office and started walking toward the cable car, he said, "This doesn't mean that I am going to die, does it?" His voice sounded very far away from my own self-absorbed fear and confusion, and I wasn't able to help or comfort him. Mechanically I said, "Of course you are not going to die. You are way too young to die. How can you even think that? But let's not talk about it right now. You need to get your mind on something else." Soon after that, Michael went back home to his parents' house in Connecticut, and I never saw him again. A year later I heard that he had died. I felt terrible remorse for not having been able to be a friend to him at a time when it mattered so much.

When someone receives a terminal diagnosis, loved ones and friends often feel awkward and uncomfortable and may even arrange a hasty retreat in order to avoid a confrontation with their own dread of death. Such distancing deprives people of the support and understanding they need. Imagine how lonely it would feel to receive a terminal diagnosis and have your friends turn away in fright. Even if you are intensely afraid, you can still be of support to a person who has received a terminal diagnosis just by remaining open to the present.

There is no way to predict exactly how someone is going to respond to the news of a terminal illness. The feelings that arise—from disbelief to fear, anger, and sadness—can be overwhelming and confusing. When my brother was given a terminal diagnosis, for several days I could do nothing for him because of my own inner turmoil. He was such a pivotal person in my life that to think of his being gone forever paralyzed me completely. Nor could I even begin to comprehend what he was going through, since I didn't even understand my own beliefs about death. To escape this uncomfortable situation, I raced away distraught—thinking only of myself, not of him. I even felt anger toward Wheeler for getting sick! Why did he have to smoke so much? Why hadn't he paid more attention to the stress in his life? Why did he have to have a *terminal* illness? At the same time, my heart ached for him and I felt powerless to be of any help.

A terminal diagnosis, whether it is one's own or that of a loved one, tells us at the most visceral level that death is certain. A person who has contemplated the certainty of death on a daily basis will be less incapacitated when forced to confront it as a personal reality. Unfortunately, to think "death is certain" contradicts the high value that most of us in the West place on permanence and fixed circumstances. When I heard that my brother's death was certain, for example, it threatened my most basic beliefs about security and tore deeply into my greatest attachments. Later, when I began to think realistically about Wheeler's death, and the certainty of any death, three questions became important to me—questions that I continue to ask myself now whenever I learn that a friend or loved one has a terminal illness:

1. What disturbs me the most when I think about my life without this person in it?
2. What is my greatest fear about this person dying?
3. What can I do to help this person right now?

Contemplating the answers to these questions helps me to distinguish between the influences of my own personal attachments in the situation and the actual needs of the person who is ill. I have found that the best way to reduce my own sadness about the impending death is to find ways to ease the suffering of the person who is ill.

At the time of hearing a terminal diagnosis, people understandably want factual information as they try to make sense of a world that seems to be slipping away. Many hope to uncover information that might contradict the terminal diagnosis, while others seek alternative opinions that may offer a more promising prognosis. All concerned need to restore some small sense of the security and safety that has suddenly been stripped away.[10] Therefore it is important for caregivers and loved ones to help the person who is ill to gather as much information as possible, reading about the condition, getting second opinions, and evaluating alternative routes of care. Many people respond with great hope that there may be a possible alternative explanation for what is happening to them, and sometimes there is. I have encountered people who are afraid they will insult their physician if they ask for a second or even a third opinion, but many physicians in fact welcome the additional input. Alternative therapies can be strong adjuncts to conventional care, and supportive techniques may significantly enhance the quality of life for the person who has been given a terminal diagnosis.[11]

When a person receives a terminal diagnosis, an awareness and acceptance of the certainty of death rarely surfaces immediately, and the first reaction of denial can sometimes prevail up to the very moment when death arrives. Even though it is unrealistic to deny the certainty of death, most people are deeply conditioned to think that life will go on indefinitely; denial is a natural and comforting response. Inner reflection is required to realize the inevitability of change and the certainty of death. People tend to rely instead on external influences such as the opinions of physicians or the beliefs of loved ones. Thus care providers who possess real knowledge and inner stability can be an invaluable source of strength and guidance. Whatever avenue a person chooses to follow after receiving a terminal diagnosis, it can be positively influenced by caregivers who are honest about their own feelings and attachments to the situation and consequently are able to be genuinely present in the face of death. To be authentic with a dying person requires open-mindedness, even though it doesn't mean that the "right" words will always come easily.

What Do I Say?
The Time of Death Is Uncertain

There is a widespread tendency in the United States to place terminally ill people in a category by themselves, as if the catastrophe of dying so estranges people from the living that they must be related to very differently and with extreme caution. It is not unusual to hear care providers as well as loved ones lament, "I just don't know what to say." One dying woman told me, "My friends are making me feel like a leper." Another one said, "They are afraid of me now—but I haven't changed." In order to breach this communication gap and reach a heartfelt connection with the dying person, caregivers and loved ones must begin to overcome their fear.

One way to overcome the dread of saying the wrong thing to a dying person is to remember that words spoken with kindness and compassion are seldom inappropriate. With positive intentions anyone can be with a dying person. Another way to neutralize the fear of saying something offensive in the presence of a dying person is to remember that just because the person has been given a terminal diagnosis does not guarantee that he or she will die before you do. People with terminal illness are no different than anyone else when it comes to the time of death being uncertain.

In my work with the dying, especially when it has been someone very close to me, the biggest barrier I have repeatedly faced has been my self-centered concern about losing the person from my own life. Feelings of sadness about the impending loss have at times caused painful and uncomfortable feelings that deeply affected my ability to relate to the dying person. An example that comes to mind was an experience I had several weeks before my brother died. One day Wheeler said to me, "I have to ask you a question, and I want you to promise that you will tell me the truth." His urgent tone immediately put me on the defensive. I kept my eyes down because I knew he was going to ask me something awkward, something threatening. "Okay," I said, "I'll do my best."

"Am I going to die?" he blurted out.

"Oh, no!" I thought, as my gut wrenched and my face flushed in embarrassment. "He must be trying to trick me. He must know that he is dying. How could he not know after what the physician has implied, the failed treatments, the increasing pain, and the persistently enlarging tumor bulging out of his chest?" All outward indications led me to believe that Wheeler was dying. He was so weak and sallow; his frame looked like a plastic skeleton. But I didn't know for sure what was going to happen. I didn't want him to die—and maybe he *wouldn't* die; how could I know? Yet to respond to him by saying, "I don't know" or "I don't want you to die" seemed inept, even silly, so instead I said, "Yes, I think you are going to die."

He looked at me with an incredulous expression that quickly turned to anger. "Well, hell," he said, "you don't have to be so damn blunt about it, do you?" Immediately I realized that I had hurt him. I felt horrible about it. Suddenly there was discord between us. It wasn't the words that I said, but the way that I had said them. My own defensiveness and fears had caused me to react with guarded self-concern. Had I been better prepared, I could have stopped acting from a position of separation and started opening myself up to the possibility of empathizing with his situation. Had I been unafraid to connect with him at a deeply primordial level, I could have taken the time to sit and face death with him and really listen to him from within. Herbert Guenther points out that " 'inner' hearing, by its very *inner*ness," can dissolve separation, and that "in the act of listening the experiencer not only opens himself up to another presence, but also allows himself to be affected by this presence."[12] To listen rather than talk, to allow silence to have its place, takes a degree of inner confidence that can be developed and will be of benefit to everyone involved. When at a loss for words, a person is not required to say anything. It is usually of little help to initiate a conversation designed to camouflage powerful feelings. Genuine solace can be expressed just by being receptive even when no words are spoken.

What's most important is to be receptive around death, to have an open mind whether the conversation turns to the topic of death or not. Some dying people have little interest in talking about death. Even people who are not in denial may refrain from discussing their situation in depth. I have found that dying people are most comfortable when they are allowed to determine the direction that the conversation takes and to maintain control over how deep it goes. A dying person deserves this freedom, and a caregiver must have enough inner confidence to resonate with empathy to any situation. A quick way to begin developing some inner confidence around death is to contemplate such questions as the following:

1. At what age do I consider death to be premature?
2. How much time do I think I have left to live?
3. What do I believe will cause my death?
4. If I died unexpectedly now, what unfinished business would I leave?
5. If I were dying, how would I want people to relate to me?
6. What do I imagine would be uncomfortable to talk about if I were dying?

It is possible to remain hopeful, courageous, and unafraid even in the face of life's greatest unknown, its closing chapter. A caregiver who has developed self-understanding is best prepared for the task. Such a caregiver is able to focus and adapt the care to meet the particular needs of the individual who is dying.

Focusing: At Death Only the Condition of the Mind Has Value

Because of sweeping changes in health-care delivery today, more and more people are dying at home, no longer hidden from view in the sterile seclusion of a hospital room. Caregivers are often loved ones or friends who have little or no experience caring for a dying person. Even if hospice services are provided in the home, some friend or family member must serve as the primary caregiver.[13] Hospice can guide, educate, and support the patient and the others involved, but the responsibility for ongoing daily care belongs to the family and friends.

Necessary tasks such as maintaining a daily schedule, providing medications, meals, and personal care can usually be performed by most people without too much difficulty. Once these basic needs have been met, however, other, higher needs may begin to emerge that are more difficult for a caregiver to fulfill. Sometimes, for example, a dying person comes to the realization that it is no longer necessary to be limited by the struggle to fully maintain conditions as if they are permanent. This attitude of less attachment is a more flexible perspective; it reflects a condition of mind that has greater resilience and is open to deeper experience, including the transpersonal dimension. Such a mental shift from the mundane to more subtle levels of communication can be disheartening for people who are frightened and confused by the existential questions that may come to the fore. For care providers who have developed death awareness, however, it can mean an exhilarating experience of growth and change for themselves as well as for their patients.

Many dying people simply want permission to die and need reassurance that their loved ones will be cared for after the parting. Caregivers who are afraid of the impending loss will not be able to genuinely offer such permission and reassurance, since they are too uncomfortable to allow such a discussion to take place. Instead, they may respond with "You're fine," "You look better today," "Don't talk about depressing things," or "Snap out of your dark mood; you could live to be a hundred." On the other hand, a caregiver who is less fearful can actually help the dying person by saying something like "I will miss your presence, but when it is time for you to go I will understand."

In the Tibetan Buddhist death meditation it is said that the only thing a person has of value at the time of death is mental conditioning and therefore it follows that dying is a time for developing peace within the mind. And in the West dying has sometimes been called the final stage of growth,[14] a time when emotional, mental, and spiritual development can be greatly accelerated. In both views, the state of the dying person's inner world is considered to be of greatest value. Caregivers contribute strongly to the complexion of a dying process, and those who have an open mind and are empathetic can positively guide the dying person toward inner peace. Accompanying a person along the dying trajectory can be a challenging undertaking, but it also has the potential for being a richly rewarding experience. As one ministers to the terminally ill, brilliant treasures of compassion, understanding, transformation, and illumination await discovery. Such treasures have been glimpsed by many caregivers at various points during the dying process. They can provide the positive energy that sustains morale and fortitude when stress or hopelessness becomes overpowering. Caregivers who have developed a transpersonal stance are able to understand that adversity can be a repository of insight and wisdom, for both patient and caregiver.

7

Developing a
Transpersonal Stance
in Care of the Dying

> Let the mind be enlarged, according to its
> capacity, to the grandeur of the mysteries,
> and not the mysteries contracted to the
> narrowness of the mind.
>
> — FRANCIS BACON,
> Advancement of Knowledge

THERE IS NO CURE FOR DEATH. DESPITE modern medicine's brilliant innovations, death inevitably brings each life to its final end. But is death really final? Tibetan Buddhism teaches that there are realities, states of consciousness, beyond the confines of the physical body and the ordinary mind. Tibetan Buddhists believe there are many subtle mind states that lie beyond ordinary consciousness, and one of them is so subtle that it is never extinguished: the mind of clear light that continues from one lifetime to the next. When the physical body dies, "there is continuation," says the fourteenth Dalai Lama. "Death involves the grosser level of the body. The subtle body still will be there."[1]

Most people have an almost instinctual sense that there is a broader consciousness that transcends "this skin sack we call our 'selves,'"[2] a consciousness not limited by the body and the ordinary mind. People who have had near-death experiences, and other individuals who have had experiences of expanded awareness—for example, Maslow's "self-actualizers"[3]—speak of having encountered a realm of human consciousness beyond the rational mind and physical reality. The experience of "other ways of knowing"[4] that transcend the limits of the ordinary mind may be why, to use Ken Wilber's words, "so many people who consistently practice some form of transpersonal 'therapy' report that they no longer really fear death."[5] During deep meditation, for example, the mind is said to rest within a transcendental reality that lies beyond the confines of physical boundaries and death.

According to Tibetan Buddhism, both life and death are states of being. The after-death state begins when the mind-continuum separates from the body at death and doesn't end until the mind-continuum enters a new rebirth. The state of being constantly changes from moment to moment and from lifetime to lifetime, yet it remains connected by an individual thread of continuity that streams through it. The Dalai Lama explains:

> The self exists in the former lifetime, exists in this lifetime, and will exist in the next lifetime. Yesterday's *I* and today's *I* and tomorrow's *I* are in a sense the same *I*, but in another sense, yesterday's *I* is no more; it is already gone, and tomorrow's *I* is yet to come. But as a whole, the continuum of the *I* moment by moment extends through the whole process.[6]

Receptivity to the transpersonal dimension during the dying trajectory is important for loved ones and care providers because it increases their potential for moving beyond the limiting sense of impending loss that can stifle happiness. It is impossible to completely avoid the pain of loss that death brings, but it is possible to reconstruct the experience in such a way that brings comfort and peace to everyone involved. Care providers and loved ones who try to replace their old mental habits of prejudice and antipathy about death with more realistic and spontaneous responses can begin to deepen their understanding and view an individual death within a broader context, one in which death is seen as the universal suffering that all mortals equally endure. This recognition produces a strong sense of empathy and compassion for everyone. And out of this empathy and compassion a confident presence around death naturally begins to develop—a presence that can serve as a wellspring of strength and illumination throughout the dying process.

Presence, Not Pretense

Unfortunately pretense is the common practice around a person who is close to death. Florence Nightingale wrote about the many times she had observed people thoughtlessly assailing a person near death with falsities such as "I am glad to see you looking so well, why don't you take a little more exercise and amusement?"[7] Evading the truth may help to circumvent a confrontation with death for the caregiver or loved one, but it does little to improve conditions for the dying person. Even if they do not openly acknowledge it, most people seem to intuitively know when they are dying;[8] attempts to deceive them are not only unkind but also transparent, especially as the final days approach.

A person who has presence around death will face it and encounter a dying person with open-mindedness and honesty. As care providers and loved ones replace subjective fears and preconceptions with genuine compassion for the dying, presence develops. A part of that presence is empathy—a willingness to step into the dying person's shoes and see the situation from that perspective. If you can imagine that you yourself are dying (a psychological challenge in and of itself), it will help you answer the first two questions below before taking up the third and most crucial step.

1. If I were terminally ill, who of those I know would I like to provide my care?
2. What personal qualities do I consider the most valuable in care providers?
3. What qualities do I need to cultivate in order to be like my ideal care provider?

Although people might wish for any number of qualities in a care provider, most agree that respect and compassion are the most valuable. When a person providing care is neither frightened of death nor estranged by a lack of appreciation for the transpersonal, respect and compassion come naturally. Care providers who hold a transpersonal perspective and who have developed death awareness are in a position to empower the dying by legitimizing their experiences. On the other hand, a lack of death awareness can limit the experience of dying to a personal tragedy, to nothing more than pain, grief, and hopelessness. Instead of ignoring or acquiescing to discouragement, a care provider or loved one who has developed a transpersonal presence can guide a dying person out of the shadows of sadness and pessimism and help map out ways to strive for inner peace. Drawing upon a number of methods, from relaxation techniques to formal meditations, a care provider can find the appropriate means to maintain a relaxed and healing atmosphere for the dying person.[9]

Toward the end of his own life, psychologist Abraham Maslow speculated that death awareness can produce "the transcendent, transpersonal, transhuman."[10] A care provider who has developed death awareness is able to provide an open, nurturant, and fertile environment to help actualize the fullest experiential and cognitive potential of a dying person. Open-mindedness, sensitivity, and insightfulness are mental tendencies that exemplify a transpersonal stance, and thus from the transpersonal perspective, the process of dying can be viewed as an opportunity to reach unparalleled understanding and inner peace. The purpose and focus of the care provider with a transpersonal stance or presence is to facilitate a dying person's efforts to fulfill the "final stage of growth" and find harmony and peace in his or her final days.

Promoting Peace in Relationships: Forgiveness

A care provider can help a dying person reach a peaceful state of mind by promoting forgiveness in past and present relationships. Many people habitually cling to the past and store up resentment during their lifetimes,[11] but as death approaches it is important to help them let go of these disturbing tendencies and reconcile troubled relationships. Some dying people themselves express genuine urgency about mending interpersonal misunderstandings and resentments. As death's steady advance strips away the illusion of permanence, former discord often reveals itself to be pointless embitterment based on a past that has long since disappeared. One key ingredient in helping dying people to resolve unsettled relationships and forgive others as well as themselves is the caregiver's willingness to encourage and inspire. For example, if the dying person is feeling unforgiving and dwelling on past mistakes, a person providing the care can redirect that person's mind toward remembering accomplishments and other life-affirming experiences, using exercises such as the life review, or positive visualizations.

I once cared for a young woman named Jane who was dying of cancer. Although her death was drawing ominously near, she remained unable to forgive her partner, Ed, for an affair that he had had three years earlier. Both Jane and Ed were suffering deeply because of the emotional distance this unhealed wound was causing in their final journey together. Ed asked for help because he was very afraid that she would die "hating" him, and that he would feel guilty for the rest of his life. Jane, too, dearly wanted to let go of her resentment, but she didn't know how. To begin with, I taught her some deep breathing exercises to help her to relax. Then I encouraged her to talk to me about how Ed's affair had made her feel about herself. Over the next few days she began to realize that even though she had felt rejected and terribly hurt by Ed's affair, she also blamed herself for it. She cried a lot. She vented her feelings about Ed's faults and flaws but she also said "I was so cold and uncaring for a while. No wonder he sought comfort from someone else." When she recognized that in fact both of them had turned away from each other, she started to let go of her pent-up anger. As she became less guarded and tense about discussing the affair, she and Ed began to explore their motives and intentions and other events that had occurred around the incident. Their mutual openhearted and trusting self-disclosure restored the understanding that had been missing between them. Forgiveness permeated the last two weeks of Jane's life, and both she and Ed were extremely happy in each other's presence.

Relational dynamics shift when death is imminent. The knowledge that one will soon be gone from life neutralizes many of the common anxieties that undermine ordinary interactions, such as fears of betrayal or hidden agendas. Many times the rote reactions adopted in worldly exchanges are forgotten altogether, and more spontaneous responses naturally begin to take their place. Communication with a dying person can be extremely forthright, and deeply meaningful bonds can grow between the patient, the caregiver, and the others who are involved. Around a deathbed even ordinary conversations can be profoundly moving. One young woman spoke to me eloquently about her family and how close they had become during her father's death. It was a time during which they spoke to one another in extraordinarily candid and uplifting ways, achieving new intimacy. Unfortunately, everything returned to "normal" after the funeral, almost as though they forgot that they had ever become that open with one another!

As old affronts are forgiven and worldly affairs resolved, many dying people turn inward and become intolerant of shallow conversations. Dying can suddenly allow people to live in the present, transforming patients into beings with a radiant serenity and peace from within that is palpable to others. To interact dishonestly or superficially with people who've achieved this state is not appropriate. One dying woman I knew named several friends she no longer wanted to have as visitors, not because she had unresolved relationships with them, but because they were so frightened by death that they hid behind a veil of false encouragement and made her feel misunderstood, even reviled. Although she was too weak to tell them herself, I was able to intercede on her behalf and gently inform them of her true wishes. A sensitive care provider can act as the dying person's advocate and be of invaluable help in maintaining or restoring peace in relationships.

The internal mind-state is in a continually dynamic and energetic process of transformation that takes place whether a person is aware of it or not, and so relating authentically with a dying person can lead to a perspective that is less constrained by the world of conventional facts and more open to transpersonal realities. As the Buddha said, "We are but guests visiting this world, though most do not know this. Those who see the real situation no longer feel inclined to quarrel."[12]

Ensuring Peace at the End: Sacred Passage

As Dr. Sherwin Nuland tells us in his book *How We Die*, "Every life is different from any that has gone before it, and so is every death."[13] There will always be vast individual differences in the emotional and spiritual dimensions of a dying trajectory. However, as "Time's winged chariot hurries near" (in the words of the English poet Andrew Marvell), there will also be observably similar physical patterns such as those identified in the eight stages of dissolution leading to death. Some dying people will talk openly about angels or other heavenly figures who visit them; it is not uncommon for people who are very close to death to actually fall out of bed trying to reach some force that others are unable to see.[14] It is almost as if the dying "live between two worlds . . . no longer at home in this one, not yet secure in the next."[15]

To surround the dying person with lovingkindness in thought, word, and deed is essential if a measure of peace during the dying process is to be ensured. During the last hours of someone's life, friends at the bedside may be overwhelmed by the urge to be very active in order to escape emotionally and mentally. Others may become excessively sentimental and find themselves unable to stop crying. Dying people need to know that others are concerned, but too much disruption or sadness will only cause them to suffer more. Maintaining peace for the dying person's mind is of paramount importance; thus a caregiver or loved one who has developed a transpersonal presence will be better able to sit quietly at the bedside and just *be* with the dying person. These final long minutes are filled with enormous wonder for those who are not afraid to experience them. Sitting beside a person who is "actively dying" (as the palliative care profession has come to refer to this end stage) brings the present moment into intense focus. The erratic, shallow inhalations shorten and the distance between them grows until the last exhalation hovers unanswered. The onlooker feels a vast stillness, as though everything were weightless in a continuum beyond time. One moment a loved one is alive and just a moment later he or she is dead. The dying person has gone. In the extraordinarily sacred and luminous moments that follow, the way to deeper experience opens.

Those who are left behind may respond in very different ways. Although some rally great courage and fortitude from the profoundly moving experience, others do not. A resolute, calm caregiver can help those left behind to develop a more positive attitude about death by redirecting errant energies and focusing attention on the needs of the deceased. Washing the dead person's body with perfumed water, for example, is one of the most natural ceremonies that can be initiated after a death. Then family members can gather around the bed, say their prayers and good-byes, and express fond remembrances. Families vary greatly in what they want to do after a death has occurred, but most are grateful for any guidance and direction that helps them reach a sense of closure.

The power of the mind is extraordinary. With our mind we make our world. The mind—the ground of both life and death— is an inner treasure of clarity and self-understanding that we can draw upon, even to ease the suffering of death. Yet, sad to say, it is an inner treasure often recognized only in extremity. But the treasure is always there, its discovery imminent in any moment. It is not dying that reveals it, but awakening.

NOTES

Introduction

1. Dane Rudhyar, *Rhythm of Wholeness: A Total Affirmation of Being* (Wheaton, Ill.: Theosophical Publishing House, 1983), p. 219.
2. See Herbert Benson et al., "Three Case Reports of the Metabolic and Electroencephalographic Changes During Advanced Buddhist Meditation Techniques," *Behavioral Medicine* 16:2 (1990): 90–95.
3. See Gary G. E. Schwartz, "Psychophysiology of Imagery and Healing: A Systems Perspective," in *Imagination and Healing*, ed. Anees A. Sheikh (Farmingdale, N.Y.: Baywood, 1984), pp. 35–50.
4. See Herbert Benson, *The Relaxation Response* (New York: Avon Books, 1976).
5. The life review is a process wherein individuals recall and recast the events of their life within the context of their current understanding. The process of reviewing one's life is not only a naturally occurring activity but also seems to help individuals, especially later in life, to make significant gains in their sense of life satisfaction and psychological well-being.

Chapter 1. The Problem of Death Denial

1. There is nothing wrong with seeking as much experimental treatment as the dying person wants, but to push aggressive treatments when the dying person no longer wants them can be inappropriate.
2. Morrie Schwartz, *Letting Go: Morrie's Reflections on Living while Dying* (New York: Walker and Co., 1997), p. 78.
3. See Robert Fulton and Greg Owen, "Death in Contemporary American Society," in *Death and Identity*, ed. Robert Fulton and Robert Bendiksen, 3d ed. (Philadelphia: Charles Press, 1994), pp. 12–27.
4. For reports of early studies about life-support techniques, see C. G. Engstrom, "Treatment of Severe Respiratory Paralysis by the Engstrom Universal Respirator," *British Medical Journal* 2 (1954): 666. See also P. Zoll et al., "Termination of Ventricular Fibrillation in Many by Externally Applied Electric Countershock," *New England Journal of Medicine* 254 (1956): 727. See also W. B. Kouwenhoven, J. R. Jude, G. G. Knickerbocker, "Closed-Chest Cardiac Massage," *Journal of the American Medical Association* 173 (1960): 1064.
5. Many studies report these statistics; for example, see Judith A. Levy, "The Hospice in the Context of an Aging Society," in Fulton and Bendiksen, *Death and Identity*, pp. 364–381.
6. For example, see G. E. Dickinson and R. E. Tournier, "A Decade beyond Medical School: A Longitudinal Study of Physicians' Attitudes toward Death and Terminally Ill Patients," *Social Science and Medicine* 38 (1994): 1397–1400. See also Jean J. E. Kincade, "Attitudes Of Physicians, House-staff, and Nurses on Care for the Terminally Ill," *Omega, Journal of Death and Dying* 13 (1982): 333–344.
7. For example, see L. M. Kopelman, "Philosophy and Medical Education," *Academic Medicine* 70 (1995): 795–805. See also Alan C. Mermann, "Learning to Care for the Dying," in Howard M. Spiro, Mary G. McCrea Curnen, and Lee Palmer Wandel, eds., *Facing Death: Where Culture, Religion, and Medicine Meet* (New Haven: Yale University Press, 1996), pp. 52–59.
8. See Jacqueline Flaskerud et al., "Avoidance and Distancing: A Descriptive View of Nursing," *Nursing Forum* 18:2 (1979): 158–175. See also S. Wilkinson, "Factors Which Influence How Nurses Communicate with Cancer Patients," *Journal of Advanced Nursing* 16 (1991): 677–688.

9. Florence Nightingale, *Notes on Nursing: What It Is and What It Is Not* (1860; reprint, New York: Dover Publications, 1969), p. 96.

10. Elisabeth Kübler-Ross, *Death: The Final Stage of Growth* (Englewood Cliffs, N.J.: Prentice-Hall, 1975), p. 6.

11. According to the *New York Times Almanac* (New York: Penguin, 1999), close to 1.6 million people were cared for in approximately 16,800 nursing homes in the United States in the late 1990s. In 1996, Americans spent $78.5 billion on nursing home care, up from $800 million in 1996.

12. My visit to this nursing home was in the late 1970s, before advance directives such as a living will, were legalized. In a living will, a person specifies in writing what kinds of treatment are wanted and not wanted if he or she should fall into a persistent vegetative state or otherwise not be able to make health-care decisions. It wasn't until the last decade of the twentieth century that the living will became a law in all the states. There are arguments that the living will is virtually useless since medications and treatments are developing and changing so rapidly that a person can't really know in advance what his or her particular medical situation will require. However, the living will does provide much needed guidelines for caregivers and loved ones who are caring for patients who are no longer able to communicate what they want.

13. Many people are under the impression that hospice care only takes place in a facility. However, hospices often deliver services directly to the patient in his or her own home, although in order to qualify for at-home hospice service the patient must also have a primary caregiver in the home.

Chapter 2. A Broader View of Healing

1. For an in-depth discussion of the stages of dying, see Elisabeth Kübler-Ross, *Death: The Final Stage of Growth* (Englewood Cliffs, N.J.: Prentice-Hall, 1975).

2. *Transpersonal* combines *trans*, meaning "through, across, from one place to another, beyond the ordinary limits of," and *personal*, meaning "separate, private, individual." *Transpersonal* thus means beyond

an individual sense of a separate identity, one that is limited within a self-defined boundary, apart from others. Transpersonal experiences occur when an individual transcends the merely personal and identifies instead with the interconnectedness of the entire universe. Transpersonal studies are concerned with the recognition of humanity's highest potential and with the "recognition, understanding, and realization of unitive, spiritual, and transcendent states of consciousness." See Denise LaJoie and Sam I. Shapiro, "Definitions of Transpersonal Psychology: The First Twenty-three Years," *Journal of Transpersonal Psychology* 24(1992): 79–98.

3. See Ira Byock, *Dying Well: Peace and Possibilities at the End of Life* (New York: Riverhead Books, 1997).

4. Hospice care is palliative care. People are eligible for hospice care when there is no further curative treatment available for their disease and their physician has given them a diagnosis of six months or less to live. Key goals of hospice care are to help a person achieve a peaceful and dignified death. For more about hospice, see Sandol Stoddard, *The Hospice Movement: A Better Way of Caring for the Dying*, rev. ed. (New York: Vintage Books, 1991). See also Florence Wald, "The Emergence of Hospice Care in the United States," in Howard M. Spiro et al., *Facing Death: Where Culture, Religion, and Medicine Meet*, pp. 81–89.

5. The first American hospice was started in Connecticut in 1974 under the direction of nurse Florence Wald.

6. For example, the cover of the March 17, 1997, issue of *U.S. News and World Report* carried the following caption: *No excuse for pain: New science, old thinking. Doctors have the means at hand to relieve the suffering of millions of Americans. Why aren't they doing it?*

7. For example, see G. Frank Lawlis, ed., *Transpersonal Medicine: The New Approach to Healing Body-Mind-Spirit* (Boston: Shambhala Publications, 1996).

8. See Herbert Benson, *Beyond the Relaxation Response* (New York: Times Books, 1984).

9. Brain-wave measurements indicate that the daily awake state produces an amplitude of beta waves between 13 and 26 hertz, a relaxed and calm state produces an amplitude of alpha waves between 8 and

13 hertz, and a state of deep relaxation such as just prior to sleep produces an amplitude of theta waves between 4 and 8 hertz. The average person cannot maintain theta waves without falling asleep, though a meditator can. During sleep or unconsciousness, delta waves are present at 0.5 to 4 hertz.

10. Herbert Benson, M.D., testimony on healing and the mind before the United States House of Representatives, November 5, 1997.

11. See Harris Dienstfrey (ed.), *Where the Body Meets the Mind: Type A, the Relaxation Response, Psychoneuroimmunology, Biofeedback, Neuropeptides, Hypnosis, Imagery, and the Search for the Mind's Effect on Physical Health* (New York: HarperPerennial, 1991). See also G. F. Solomon, "Whither Psychoneuroimmunology? A New Era of Immunology, of Psychosomatic Medicine, and of Neuroscience," *Brain, Behavior, and Immunity* 7 (1993): 352–366.

12. For example, see Robert Ader and Nicholas Cohen, "Behaviorally Conditioned Immunosuppression," *Psychosomatic Medicine* 37 (1975): 333–340, and "Psychoneuroimmunology: Conditioning and Stress," *Annual Review of Psychology* 44 (1993): 53–85. Also see L. S. Berk et al., "Neuroendocrine and Stress Hormone Changes During Mirthful Laughter," *American Journal of Medical Sciences* 29 (1989): 390–396.

13. Candace B. Pert, "Neuropeptides, AIDS, and the Science of Mind-Body Healing," *Alternative Therapies* 1:3 (1995): 71–76.

14. See Norman Cousins, "Belief Becomes Biology," *Advances, The Journal of Mind-Body Health* 6:3 (1989): 20–29. See also Cousins's well-known story of his own experience, *Anatomy of an Illness: As Perceived by the Patient* (New York: Bantam, 1991).

15. See Lee Jussim, "Self-Fulfilling Prophecies: A Theoretical and Integrative Review," *Psychological Review* 93 (1986): 429–445.

16. See Blair Justice, *Who Gets Sick: How Beliefs, Moods, and Thoughts Affect Your Health* (Los Angeles: Jeremy P. Tarcher, 1987), pp. 273–286.

17. Victor E. Frankl, *Man's Search for Meaning*, rev. ed. (New York: Washington Square Press, 1984), p. 57.

18. For further discussion about remission and healing, see Herbert Benson, *Timeless Healing: The Power and Biology of Belief* (New

York: Scribner, 1996). See also Andrew Weil, *Spontaneous Healing: How to Discover and Enhance Your Body's Natural Ability to Maintain and Heal Itself* (New York: Ballantine Books, 1996).

19. For more about holistic nursing and the use of visualization in healing, see Barbara Dossey et al., *Holistic Nursing: A Handbook for Practice* (Rockville, Md.: Aspen, 2nd ed., 1995).

20. Francis Galton's original study, "Statistical Inquiries into the Efficacy of Prayer," was published in 1872, in the *Fortnightly Review*, an English journal established as vehicle for the expression of advanced liberal views.

21. For example, see Larry Dossey, *Healing Words: The Power of Prayer and the Practice of Medicine* (San Francisco: HarperSanFrancisco, 1993).

22. Stephen Levine, *Who Dies? An Investigation of Conscious Living and Conscious Dying* (Garden City, N.Y.: Doubleday, Anchor Press, 1982), p. 59.

Chapter 3. Awakening to Impermanence and Facing Death

1. Elisabeth Kübler-Ross, *Death: The Final Stage of Growth* (Englewood Cliffs, N.J.: Prentice-Hall, 1975), p. 164.

Chapter 4. Ceaseless Transformation

1. Paltrul Rinpoche, *Kunzang lama'i Shelung: The Words of My Perfect Teacher*, trans. Padmakara Translation Group (Boston: Shambhala Publications, 1998), p. 46.

2. Robert A. F. Thurman, trans., *The Tibetan Book of the Dead: Liberation through Understanding in the Between* (New York: Bantam Book, 1994), p. 20.

3. *Dhammapada*, trans. Dharma Publishing Staff (Oakland: Dharma Publishing, 1985), p. 108.

4. Paltrul Rinpoche, *The Words of My Perfect Teacher*, p. 119.

5. *Dhammapada*, p. 123.

6. Lama Thubten Yeshe, *The Tantric Path of Purification: The Yoga*

Method of Heruka Vajrasattva (Boston: Wisdom Publications, 1995), p. 9.

7. *Bodhicitta* literally means "enlightened [*bodhi*] mind [*citta*]." An enlightened mind is free from bias and therefore able to see all beings as equal. To view beings as equal, according to Tibetan Buddhism, generates the altruistic and compassionate aspiration to liberate all sentient beings from suffering—that is, to liberate all beings from rebirth in cyclic existence.

8. His Holiness the Dalai Lama, *Beyond Dogma: Dialogues and Discourses*, trans. Alison Anderson (Berkeley: North Atlantic Books, 1996), p. 194.

9. Geshe Rabten, *The Essential Nectar*, p. 92.

10. See Kalu Rinpoche, *The Dharma That Illuminates All Beings Impartially Like the Light of the Sun and the Moon*, trans. Janet Gyatso. (Albany: State University of New York Press, 1986), pp. 117–118.

11. Tilopa, quoted in Kalu Rinpoche, *Luminous Mind: The Way of the Buddha* (Boston: Wisdom Publications, 1992), p. 193. A *kalpa* is the life cycle of a universe.

12. His Holiness the Dalai Lama, *Beyond Dogma*, p. 227.

13. Tilopa, quoted in Herbert V. Guenther, *The Life and Teaching of Naropa* (Boston: Shambhala Publications, 1986), p. 193.

14. The child and mother analogy is often found in Tibetan Buddhist accounts of what happens at the moment of death. For example, see Lama Lodö, *Bardo Teachings: The Way of Death and Rebirth*, rev. ed. (San Francisco: KDK Publications, 1982); also Chagdud Tülku Rinpoche, *Life in Relation to Death* (Cottage Grove, Ore.: Padma, 1987).

15. In Tibet, a tradition has evolved around the discovery of buried treasures called *terma*. Terma can be found internally, imbedded in the mind, or they can be found in external places. The original ancient terma custom began as the Tibetan practice of burying politically sensitive material to protect it from enemies. The terma tradition evolved to include buried treasures such as religious objects and statues and instructional texts that were discovered in the ground or in monastery walls, or heard spoken from trees, caves, or out of the sky. Discoverers of the treasure texts are called *tertön*, the preordained bearers of a fresh presentation of specific teachings, and

demonstrate the metaphoric creativity of the terma tradition in allowing existing teachings to be rediscovered and revitalized when changing situations require a new vision. Tülku Thondup provides some photographs of terma in his book *Hidden Teachings of Tibet: An Explanation of the Terma Tradition of the Nyingma School of Buddhism* (London: Wisdom Publications, 1986).

16. Geshe Rabten, *The Essential Nectar: Meditations on the Buddhist Path*, trans. Martin Willson (London: Wisdom Publications, 1984), p. 67.

17. The most subtle essence of the mind—referred to as the mind-continuum in this book—is sometimes referred to as the awareness principle, the stream of consciousness, the mind stream, the mind-essence, the essence of awakening, or pure awareness.

18. W. Y. Evans-Wentz, trans., *The Tibetan Book of the Dead: Or the After-Death Experiences on the Bardo Plane, According to Lama Kazi Dawa-Samdup's English Rendering*, 3d ed. (London: Oxford University Press, 1957), p. 30.

19. In *Opening the Eye of New Awareness* (Boston: Wisdom Publications, 1985), p. 17.

20. The Dalai Lama is said to be an incarnation of Avalokiteshvara, also called the Bodhisattva of Compassion. Bodhisattvas are beings who have attained understanding about the true nature of reality and are advanced on the path to liberation from cyclic existence. Out of compassion for other beings, they continue to reincarnate in order to help others realize freedom from rebirth. The first Dalai Lama, Gendün Drub, was born in the late fourteenth century, and since then is said to have reincarnated thirteen times. The current and fourteenth Dalai Lama, Tenzin Gyatso, escaped from Tibet to India in 1959, when it became tragically and irreversibly clear that the Chinese were intent on destroying Tibetan culture. Through his extensive teaching, writing, and travel, he has become known as a major spokesman of universal responsibility and nonviolence, even in the face of aggression. For his service to the cause of world peace, he was awarded the Nobel Peace Prize in 1989.

The Karmapa is the spiritual authority of the Karma Kagyü school of Tibetan Buddhism. The first Karmapa, prior to his death in the thirteenth century, wrote a letter describing the circumstances of where and when he would be reborn. He became the first enlightened teacher to predict the time and place of his chosen rebirth in this way. The Karmapas are also known as the Black Hat Lamas because during the fifteenth century the emperor of China had a dream about a hat floating over the Karmapa's head. The emperor had a replica of the hat made that he presented to the fifth Karmapa and the Black Hat Ceremony was established. During the ceremony, a transmission of inner realization from the master to the disciple—the cutting through self-deception so that the Buddha mind can be born—will occur if the student has sufficient devotion.

21. In this case, reincarnation means that the person actually chooses the time, place, and parents for the future rebirth, rather than experiencing rebirth at the mercy of karmic tendency.

22. For a brief overview of the current Dalai Lama's perspective regarding arguments for rebirth, see Tenzin Gyatso, the Fourteenth Dalai Lama, *The World of Tibetan Buddhism: An Overview of Its Philosophy and Practice,* trans. Geshe Thupten Jinpa (Boston: Wisdom Publications, 1995), pp. 47–49. See also his earlier work *Opening the Eye of New Awareness,* trans. Donald S. Lopez, Jr. (Boston: Wisdom Publications, 1985), pp. 34–38.

23. The six realms of existence are as follows:

The realm of hell-beings: There are many different hells, some red hot, some ice cold, some cutting, some crushing. All the hells are characterized by violence and aggression, and rebirth into any one of them is the result of former evil actions and strong tendencies toward anger and hatred.

The realm of ghosts: The ghost realm is characterized by intense greed: a person is propelled to the ghost realm by strong attachments and desires. It is said that certain people in this realm appear in a form similar to their previous one and can sometimes be seen by humans.

The realm of animals: The animal realm is characterized by ignorance: a person is drawn there by sloth and small-mindedness. Animals, like humans, develop deep attachments and feel anger, pride, and jealousy. But animals have little power to reason, and their stupidity forces them to accept whatever mistreatment and unkindness they are shown.

The human realm: The human realm is characterized by both pleasure and pain. Although there are many kinds of enjoyment in the human realm, there is also the inescapable suffering brought about by birth, aging, sickness, and death.

The demigod realm: The realm of the demigods is characterized by jealousy and fighting. These beings, who outwardly appear as gods, are inwardly consumed by intense jealousy of the god realm that they can see unfolding around them. The good fortune of beings in the god realm is intolerable to the demigods because they are unable to bear the advantages of others; as a consequence, their existence is filled with constant dissatisfaction.

The god realm: The god realm is characterized by comfort and beauty, but it also tainted by the painful awareness that such happiness is only temporary. Fears about losing the fortuitous conditions establish negative tendencies that lead the god being to rebirth in a less fortunate realm.

24. Detlef I. Lauf, *Secret Doctrines of the Tibetan Books of the Dead*, trans. Graham Parkes (Boston: Shambhala Publications, 1989), p. 228.

25. See, for example, *The Tibetan Book of the Dead: The Great Liberation through Hearing in the Bardo* trans. Francesca Fremantle and Chögyam Trungpa (Boston: Shambhala Publications, 1987) and *The Tibetan Book of the Dead*, trans. Robert A. F. Thurman (New York: Bantam, Books 1994).

26. In Tibetan *bar* means "between," and *do* means "two." In general, *bardo* means any interval, but in the West the word *bardo* is understood more specifically as referring to the interval between death and rebirth.

27. As the days progress in the *bardo*, "the radiances of the higher nature fade into the lights of the lower nature." As karmic tendencies slowly reappear, the deceased is led away from the vision of the sublime, purified universe toward rebirth into one of the realms of cyclic existence. See W. Y. Evans-Wentz, *The Tibetan Book of the Dead*, p. 17.

28. Tsele Natsok Rangdröl, *The Mirror of Mindfulness: The Cycle of the Four Bardos*, trans. Erik Pema Kunsang (Boston: Shambhala Publications, 1989), p. 52.

29. In the context of the *bardo*, time is relative. A day it is variously described as being as long as a day, as long as it takes to eat a meal, or as long as a hand clap. It is also described as "the duration of nondistraction from mind-essence." (See Tsele Natsok Rangdröl, *The Mirror of Mindfulness*, p. 4).

30. W. Y. Evans-Wentz, *The Tibetan Book of the Dead*, p. 31.

31. Sogyal Rinpoche, *The Tibetan Book of Living and Dying*, p. 276.

32. Each realm has a murky, dull-colored light that beckons to the mind-continuum: a dull white light from the god realm, dull green from the demigod realm, dull yellow from the human realm, dull blue from the animal world, dull red from the ghost realm, and dull smoke-colored light from the hell realm. See W. Y. Evans-Wentz, *The Tibetan Book of the Dead*, pp. 173–174.

33. Adapted primarily from (1) the text of monks chanting at the bedside of a dying person in a film by Graham Coleman and David Lascelles, *A Tibetan Trilogy, Part 2: The Fields of the Senses* (Seattle: ThreadCross Films, 1993), and (2) Lama Lodö, *Bardo Teachings: The Way of Death and Rebirth*, rev. ed. (San Francisco: KDK Publications, 1982), pp. 21–48.

34. The Fourteenth Dalai Lama, His Holiness Tenzin Gyatso, *Kindness, Clarity, and Insight*, trans. and ed. Jeffrey Hopkins (Ithaca, N.Y.: Snow Lion Publications, 1984), p. 181.

35. Robert A. F. Thurman, *The Tibetan Book of the Dead: Liberation through Understanding in the Between* (New York: Bantam Books, 1994), p. xxi.

Chapter 5. The Eight Stages of Dissolution

1. For an in-depth discussion about the elements that compose the body, see Tom Dummer, *Tibetan Medicine and Other Holistic Health-Care Systems* (New Delhi: Paljor, 1994), pp. 8–50.

2. According to Tibetan tradition, it is not just in dying that the dissolutions occur; they also happen naturally when falling asleep. The dissolution of the elements can also be brought about by a specific meditation that uses imagination and concentration. The dissolution of the elements whether occurring naturally, as in dying or falling

asleep, or through concentration, as in a very specific meditation, causes a shift in consciousness from a gross to a more subtle level.

3. "Or perhaps not at all, which would be most unfortunate," according to Ven. Karma Lekshe Tsomo (personal communication, January 1997).

4. The description of the stages of dissolution leading to death is based on material found primarily in (1) Lati Rinbochay and Jeffrey Hopkins, *Death, Intermediate State and Rebirth in Tibetan Buddhism* (Ithaca, N.Y.: Snow Lion Publications, 1979), pp. 13–57; (2) Terry Clifford, *Tibetan Buddhist Medicine and Psychiatry: The Diamond Healing* (York Beach, Me.: Samuel Weiser, 1984), pp. 108–114; and (3) Kalu Rinpoche, *Luminous Mind: The Way of the Buddha* (Boston: Wisdom Publications, 1997), pp. 53–56.

5. In the context of the eight dissolutions leading to death, the word *dissolve* does not mean that one element is actually dissolving into the other, but rather that the "dissolving" element is losing its ability to act as a "basis of consciousness." See Lati Rinbochay, *Death, Intermediate State and Rebirth in Tibetan Buddhism*, p. 38.

6. Giacomella Orofino trans., *Sacred Tibetan Teachings on Death and Liberation: Texts from the Most Ancient Traditions of Tibet* (Dorset, England: Prism Press, 1990), p. 68.

7. This is not to imply that Tibetan tradition opposes pain medication or is in favor of withholding pain medication from a person who has pain. It simply means that if a person does not have pain and does not want pain medicine, why give it?

8. Tenzin Gyatso, the Fourteenth Dalai Lama, quoted in Lati Rinbochay, *Death, Intermediate State and Rebirth in Tibetan Buddhism*, p. 8.

9. As a caregiver I have often noticed at this stage what appears to be a thickening of the tongue, but not necessarily a darkening of the tongue, although shortly after respirations cease the tongue darkens considerably.

10. Bokar Rinpoche remarks that slipping into sadness around a death is not a positive attitude since it is a focus on "feeling sorry for ourselves." What is more important is to consider the suffering of the individuals who are dying and "do what we can to relieve them." See Bokar Rinpoche, *Death and the Art of Dying in Tibetan Buddhism*,

trans. Christiane Bucher (San Francisco: ClearPoint Press, 1993), fn. 1, p. 98.

11. The Tibetan word for "drop," *thig-le*, in this context refers to the pure essence of the white/male and red/female generative or psychophysiological principles of the body. For more discussion about the drops, see Daniel Cozort, *Highest Yoga Tantra* (Ithaca, N.Y.: Snow Lion Publications, 1986); and Kalu Rinpoche, *Secret Buddhism: Vajrayana Practices* (San Francisco: ClearPoint Press, 1995).

12. Kalu Rinpoche, quoted in *Gently Whispered: Oral Teachings by the Very Venerable Kalu Rinpoche*, ed. Elizabeth Selandia (Barrytown, N.Y.: Station Hill Press, 1994), p. 75.

13. The length of time a person sees the lights of the subtle minds is said to depend on that person's spiritual awareness.

14. Lati Rinbochay and Jeffrey Hopkins, *Death, Intermediate State and Rebirth in Tibetan Buddhism*, p. 18.

15. Certain meditations are designed to increase a practitioner's ability to recognize the clear light. For example, see Glenn H. Mullin, ed. and trans., *Tsongkhapa's Six Yogas of Naropa* (Ithaca, N.Y.: Snow Lion Publications, 1996), pp. 198–208.

16. See Lati Rinbochay, *Death, Intermediate State and Rebirth in Tibetan Buddhism*, p. 19.

17. In my experience as a caregiver I have never seen the red or white signs of blood or pus appear after a person has stopped breathing.

18. For a brief explanation of the title of Karmapa, see note 20 of chapter 4 (p. 132).

19. *The Lion's Roar,* Nalanda Foundation and Centre Productions, 1985, filmstrip. Available from the Naropa Institute, 2130 Arapahoe, Boulder, Co. 80302.

20. *Ibid.*

21. Lama Yeshe was exiled from Tibet in 1959. Later, he and his student Zopa Rinpoche founded the Foundation for the Preservation of the Mahayana Tradition (FPMT), an institution that today has more than sixty teaching centers throughout the world. The foundation includes monasteries, retreat centers, hospices, and a publishing house, Wisdom Publications.

22. Lama Yeshe, quoted in Vicki Mackenzie, *Reincarnation: The Boy Lama* (Boston: Wisdom Publications, 1996), p. 61.

23. Mackenzie, *Reincarnation: The Boy Lama*, p. 68.

24. Lama Yeshe, quoted in Joseph Sharp, *Living Our Dying: A Way to the Sacred in Everyday Life* (New York: Hyperion), p. 60. Lama Yeshe's statement is a reminder that troubles are almost inevitable in the presence of sickness and death, even for a patient who is an advanced practitioner of death awareness.

25. See Francisco J. Varela (ed.), *Sleeping, Dreaming, and Dying: An Exploration of Consciousness with the Dalai Lama* (Boston: Wisdom Publications, 1997), pp. 162–164.

Chapter 6. Tibetan Buddhist Practice and the Dying Trajectory

1. The *artes moriendi* tradition appeared in the fifteenth century in the form of Christian "guidebooks" that offered priests and laymen a religious framework to use when interacting with the dying. A strong theme in the books is the advice to live each day fully as though it might be the last—not with self-indulgence, but with generosity and compassion toward others. To learn more about *artes moriendi*, see Philippe Ariès, *The Hour of Our Death* (New York: Alfred A. Knopf, 1981).

2. For a condensed set of guidelines (used by hospices) on how to understand and meet the physical needs of a terminally ill person, see Michal J. K. Galazka and Karen B. Hunter, "Hospice: Current Principles and Practices," in Sandol Stoddard, *The Hospice Movement: A Better Way of Caring*, rev. ed. (New York: Vintage Books, 1991), pp. 341–363.

3. Quoted in Kalu Rinpoche, *The Dharma That Illuminates All Beings Impartially Like the Light of the Sun and the Moon* (Albany: State University of New York Press, 1986), p. 164.

4. Chandrakirti, quoted in *Compassion in Tibetan Buddhism*, trans. Jeffrey Hopkins (Ithaca, N.Y.: Snow Lion Publications, 1980), p. 184.

5. Tenzin Gyatso, the Fourteenth Dalai Lama, *The World of Tibetan Buddhism* (Boston: Wisdom Publications, 1995), p. 86.

6. *The Hundred Thousand Songs of Milarepa*, vol. 2, trans. C. G. Chang (Boston: Shambhala Publications, 1989), p. 556.

7. *Information Please: Almanac, Atlas and Yearbook* ed. Otto Johnson, 1997 (Boston: Houghton Mifflin, 1997), p. 847.
8. Glenn H. Mullin, *Death and Dying: The Tibetan Tradition* (Boston: Arkana, 1986), p. 224.
9. Kalu Rinpoche, *The Dharma That Illuminates All Beings Impartially Like the Light of the Sun and the Moon* (Albany: State University of New York Press, 1986), p. 40.
10. One of the greatest insights of psychologist Abraham Maslow was his design of a multitiered hierarchy of motivation based on the fundamental needs of a healthy human being. Maslow's hierarchy of needs is dynamic and constantly shifting, but the need at the lowest level must always be satisfied before the ones above it can be fulfilled. Once individuals have met all their basic needs, then the higher needs for self-actualization and transcendence will emerge and become the dominant motivating force.

MASLOW'S HIERARCHY OF NEEDS
Self-actualization: higher need for living on the sacred level in everyday life without denying the bodily life; integrating the spiritual search with everyday existence
Esteem needs: basic external need for status, recognition, and attention; basic internal need for self respect, autonomy, and achievement
Social needs: basic need for affection, belonging, acceptance and friendship
Safety needs: basic need for security, and protection from emotional or physical harm
Physiological needs: basic need for food, water, shelter, clothing, and sex

11. See Andrew Weil, *Health and Healing*, rev. ed. (Boston: Houghton Mifflin, 1988). Also see Bernie Siegel, *Love, Medicine and Miracles: Lessons Learned about Self-Healing from a Surgeon's Experience with Exceptional Patients* (New York: HarperPerennial Library, 1990).
12. Herbert V. Guenther, "The Complexity of the Initial Condition," *International Journal of Transpersonal Studies* 16, no. 2 (1997): 55.

13. To receive the Medicare hospice benefit, the patient must (1) have a prognosis of less than six months to live, certified by a physician; (2) have an attending physician licensed in the state; and (3) agree, along with the physician, to palliative rather than curative treatment for the terminal illness.

14. See Elisabeth Kübler-Ross, *Death: The Final Stage of Growth* (Englewood Cliffs, N.J.: Prentice-Hall, 1975).

Chapter 7. Developing a Transpersonal Stance in Care of the Dying

1. The Dalai Lama, quoted in Jeremy W. Hayward and Francisco J. Varela, eds. *Gentle Bridges: Conversations with the Dalai Lama on the Sciences of Mind* (Boston: Shambhala Publications, 1992), p. 121. To read further about the subtle body, see Glenn H. Mullin, *Tsongkhapa's Six Yogas of Naropa* (Ithaca, N.Y.: Snow Lion, 1996), pp. 73–78.

2. John Schneider, quoted in "Interview with John Schneider, Ph.D.," in *Transpersonal Medicine: A New Approach to Healing Body-Mind Spirit*, ed. G. Frank Lawlis (Boston: Shambhala Publications, 1996), p. 176.

3. See Frank G. Goble, *The Third Force: The Psychology of Abraham Maslow* (New York: Pocket Books, 1970).

4. See John Broomfield, *Other Ways of Knowing: Recharting Our Future with Ageless Wisdom* (Rochester, Vt.: Inner Traditions International, 1997).

5. Ken Wilber, *No Boundary: Eastern and Western Approaches to Personal Growth* (Boston: Shambhala Publications, 1985), p. 135.

6. The Dalai Lama, quoted in *Dialogues with Scientists and Sages: The Search for Unity*, ed. Renée Weber (New York: Arkana, 1990), p. 238.

7. Florence Nightingale, *Notes on Nursing: What It Is and What It Is Not* (1860; reprint, New York: Dover Publications, 1969), p. 117.

8. Some dying people even seem to be able to decide when they will die. I have heard of and experienced many incidences wherein a person close to death has waited to die until after a favorite friend

arrives, a holiday has been celebrated, or some other milestone has been reached.

9. See, for example, Herbert Benson, *The Relaxation Response* (New York: Avon Books, 1976). Also see Mariah Snyder, ed., *Independent Nursing Interventions* (New York: John Wiley and Sons, 1985), pp. 47–68; and Jeanne Achterberg, *Imagery in Healing* (Boston: New Science Library, 1985).

10. See *The Journals of Abraham Maslow*, ed. Richard J. Lowry, 2 vols. (Monterey: Brooks/Cole, 1979).

11. Psychologist Abe Arkoff refers to people who behave this way as "resentment collectors." See *The Illuminated Life* (Needham Heights, Mass.: Allyn and Bacon, 1995), p. 222.

12. *Dhammapada*, trans. Dharma Publishing Staff (Oakland: Dharma Press, 1985), p. 5.

13. Sherwin B. Nuland, *How We Die: Reflections on Life's Final Chapter* (New York: Random House, Vintage Books, 1995), p. 3.

14. For example, see Maggie Callanan and Patricia Kelley, *Final Gifts: Understanding the Special Awareness, Needs, and Communications of the Dying* (New York: Bantam Books, 1992), p. 196.

15. Patricia Weenolsen, *The Art of Dying: How to Leave This World with Dignity and Grace, at Peace with Yourself and Your Loved Ones* (New York: St. Martin's Press, 1996), p. 258.

RECOMMENDED READING

Death and Dying: Western Perspectives

CALLAHAN, DANIEL. *The Troubled Dream of Life: Living with Mortality.* New York: Simon & Schuster, 1993. Examines the way we view death and how we care for the dying. Also offers insight into how to balance the rewards of modern medicine with a realistic perspective about dying.

ELIAS, NORBERT. *The Loneliness of the Dying,* trans. Edmund Jephcott. New York: Basil Blackwell, 1985. A scholarly and humane look at the emotional distance that often occurs between people who are terminally ill and their family, friends, and caregivers.

HENNEZEL, MARIE DE. *Intimate Death: How the Dying Teach Us How to Live,* trans. Carol Brown Janeway. New York: Alfred A. Knopf, 1997. Stories about patients and families facing death are told with understanding and compassion by a psychologist who works with them in a hospital for the terminally ill in France.

KASTENBAUM, ROBERT, and BEATRICE KASTENBAUM. *Encyclopedia of Death: Myth, History, Philosophy, Science.* New York: Avon Books,

1993. A concise and enlightening history of views of human mortality that ranges from ancient beliefs to modern scientific study, and includes entries from a wide variety of expert contributors.

KÜBLER-ROSS, ELISABETH. *On Death and Dying: What the Dying Have to Teach Doctors, Nurses, Clergy, and Their Own Families*. Reprint ed. New York: Simon & Schuster, 1997. This book was one of the first and most famous psychological studies on death and dying. Here Kübler-Ross introduces the five stages of confronting death: denial, anger, bargaining, depression, and acceptance.

MORGAN, ERNEST. *Dealing Creatively with Death: A Manual of Death Education and Simple Burial*. Bayside, N.Y.: Zinn Communications, 1994. Contains a wealth of useful information about such topics as memorial societies, simple burials, living wills, and bequeathal of remains to medical schools. This book delves deeply into both the practical and philosophical concerns of death and dying.

NULAND, SHERWIN B. *How We Die: Reflections on Life's Final Chapter*. New York: Random House, Vintage Books, 1995. A frank and compassionate discussion about the ways that most of us are likely to die. Dr. Nuland offers clear descriptions about many of the physiological processes that take place as dying occurs, and he also makes suggestions about how we can live more fully and meaningfully before we die.

The Spiritual Dimensions of the Dying Process

DOKA, KENNETH J., and JOHN D. MORGAN, eds. *Death and Spirituality*. Amityville, N.Y.: Baywood, 1993. Discusses many of the spiritual issues that might arise in illness and bereavement. Also suggests suitable interventions, approaches, and resources that might be useful in assisting dying people to address their spiritual needs in the face of death.

FOOS-GRABER, ANYA. *Deathing: An Intelligent Alternative for the Final Moments of Life*. Reading, Mass.: Addison-Wesley, 1984. Advocates a compassionate and open-minded approach to understanding death and dying that is both comforting and spiritually reassuring.

KAPLEAU, PHILIP. *The Zen of Living and Dying: A Practical and Spiritual Guide*. Boston: Shambhala, 1998. Examines how the cultivation of a religious orientation to dying involves, among other things, an understanding and deep acceptance of causation and the continuity of life. Offers an inspiring and illuminating look at death.

LEVINE, STEPHEN. *Who Dies? An Investigation of Conscious Living and Conscious Dying.* Garden City, N.Y.: Doubleday, Anchor Press, 1982. One of the first books actually to show the reader how to open to the positive potentials that are inherent in living with death. Written with honesty and compassion, this book greatly deepened my own understanding about death.

LONGAKER, CHRISTINE. *Facing Death and Finding Hope: A Guide to the Emotional and Spiritual Care of the Dying.* New York: Doubleday, 1997. A lovingly written guide about how to prepare for death both emotionally and spiritually using principles such as forgiveness and compassion. Can be of help to people from any spiritual tradition.

SHARP, JOSEPH. *Living Our Dying: A Way to the Sacred in Everyday Life.* ✓ New York: Hyperion, 1996. Integrating Christian, Buddhist, and contemporary cultural and psychological insights, the author, a survivor of AIDS, teaches us that death awareness cultivates a deeper appreciation for life. Personal experience described with depth of heart.

SINGH, KATHLEEN DOWLING. *The Grace in Dying: How We Are Transformed Spiritually As We Die.* ✓ San Francisco: HarperSanFrancisco, 1998. A beautifully written book that defines the stages of death in psychological and spiritual terms and delineates a path of self-discovery for the dying that leads toward transcendence.

WILBER, KEN. *Grace and Grit: Spirituality and Healing in the Life and Death of Treya Killam Wilber.* Boston: Shambhala Publications, 2000. A remarkably candid account of the many joys, sorrows, and insights experienced by a couple during their five-year struggle with the wife's cancer and her ultimate death. The clarity of Wilber's self-disclosure is very moving.

Near-Death Experiences and Life after Death

BERMAN, PHILLIP L. *The Journey Home: What Near-Death Experiences and Mysticism Teach Us about the Gift of Life.* New York: Pocket

Books, 1998. A Harvard theologian examines near-death and mystical experiences and how they can transform our lives with new meaning. Written with an inspiring appeal.

DOORE, GARY, ed. *What Survives? Contemporary Explorations of Life after Death.* Los Angeles: Jeremy P. Tarcher, 1990. A collection of writings exploring the belief in survival after death. Different perspectives are offered by many of today's leading scholars.

MOODY, RAYMOND A., JR. *Life after Life: The Investigation of a Phenomenon—Survival of Bodily Death.* New York: Bantam Books, 1975. The groundbreaking investigation presenting more than one hundred case studies of people who were revived after experiencing clinical death. Written by the physician who coined the term *near-death experience*.

MORSE, MELVIN. *Closer to the Light: Learning from the Near-Death Experiences of Children.* New York: Villard Books, 1990. A pediatrician's account of the near-death experiences reported firsthand by children who had been declared clinically dead and were then resuscitated. Although these children were too young to have previously absorbed many adult views about the near-death experience, their reports bear a remarkable similarity to those given by adults.

OSIS, KARLIS, and ERLENDUR HARALDSSON. *At the Hour of Death.* Rev. ed. New York: Hastings House, 1986. An account of modern scientific research techniques being used to investigate death and dying, and the visions of the dying. Explores the general characteristics of the apparitions seen by terminally ill patients.

RING, KENNETH, and EVELYN E. VALARINO. *Lessons from the Light: What We Can Learn from the Near-Death Experience.* Portsmouth, N.H.: Moment Point Press, 2000. An inspiring collection of near-death experiences infused with a strong sense of balance between science and human insight. The practical wisdom that is gained by people who report having had near-death experiences is explored—wisdom that has greatly diminished their fear of death.

SABOM, MICHAEL B. *Light and Death: One Doctor's Fascinating Account of Near-Death Experiences.* Grand Rapids, Mich.: Zondervan Publishing, 1998. Explores the near-death experience and death and dying from a Christian point of view.

ZALESKI, CAROL. *Otherworld Journeys: Accounts of Near-Death Experience in Medieval and Modern Times.* New York: Oxford University

Press, 1989. A comparison between near-death experiences reported in the Middles Ages and those of modern times. This fascinating study examines both the cultural and religious implications of the near-death experience and argues for the "otherworld vision" as key to understanding imaginative and religious experience.

Caregiving and Hospice

BUCKMAN, ROBERT. *I Don't Know What to Say: How to Help and Support Someone Who Is Dying.* New York: Random House, Vintage Books, 1992. A sensitive guide for friends and families of the terminally ill that not only takes some of the mystery out of the dying process, but also offers practical advice.

BYOCK, IRA. *Dying Well: Peace and Possibilities at the End of Life.* New York: Riverhead Books, 1997. These stories about terminally ill patients and their families, written by a hospice physician, are filled with the love and conciliation that is possible even in the face of pain, conflict, and dying.

CALLANAN, MAGGIE, and PATRICIA KELLEY. *Final Gifts: Understanding the Special Awareness, Needs, and Communications of the Dying.* New York: Bantam Books, 1993. Two hospice nurses share the experiences that they have had with many different dying patients. The authors provide much useful advice and make many suggestions about how caregivers and family members can better understand and respond to the special needs of people who are terminally ill.

KÜBLER-ROSS, ELISABETH. *Questions and Answers on Death and Dying.* New York: Simon & Schuster, 1997. Dr. Kübler-Ross answers the questions about death that she has most frequently been asked by doctors, nurses, patients, and others. The presentation is very down-to-earth and accessible.

NIGHTINGALE, FLORENCE. *Notes on Nursing: What It Is and What It Is Not.* 1860. Reprint. New York: Dover Publications, 1969. A collection of journal notes, from the founder of modern nursing, that reveal how the fundamental physical, emotional, and spiritual needs of the sick and the terminally ill are as similar today as they were more than 140 years ago.

SPIRO, HOWARD M., MARY G. MCREA CURNEN, and LEE PALMER WANDEL, eds. *Facing Death: Where Culture, Religion, and Medicine Meet*. New Haven, Conn.: Yale University Press, 1996. A collection of profound and eloquent reflections on medical, cultural, and religious responses to death, made by medical experts and distinguished authorities in the humanities.

STODDARD, SANDOL. *The Hospice Movement: A Better Way of Caring for the Dying*. Rev. ed. New York: Random House, 1991. An excellent reference for all who deal with the terminally ill. Outlines the way that hospice offers caring communities where dying people are treated with attention, respect, and dignity.

WEBB, MARILYN. *The Good Death: The New American Search to Reshape the End of Life*. New York: Bantam Books, 1997. Intimate portraits of dying patients that reflect the profound changes that are beginning to occur in the way Americans think about and confront death.

The Mind-Body Connection

ACHTERBERG, JEANNE, BARBARA DOSSEY, and LESLIE KOLKMEIER. *Rituals of Healing: Using Imagery for Health and Wellness*. New York: Bantam Doubleday Dell Publishing, 1994. Integrates mind-body techniques with other more traditional medical approaches for optimum healing. Included are many imagery exercises that are easy to understand and use.

BENSON, HERBERT. *Timeless Healing: The Power and Biology of Belief*. New York: Scribner, 1996. Benson, founder of Harvard's Mind/Body Institute, reports many scientific studies about the power of the mind to affect the body. He discusses not only what he calls "remembered wellness," the desire for health, but also the roles that religion, faith, and spiritual experience play in healing.

DOSSEY, LARRY. *Healing Words: The Power of Prayer and the Practice of Medicine*. San Francisco: HarperSanFrancisco, 1993. The power of prayer to heal is evaluated from a medical perspective in a way that incorporates both science and religion. The positive effects of reverence and optimism are also discussed.

GOLEMAN, DANIEL, ed. *Healing Emotions: Conversations with the Dalai Lama on Mindfulness, Emotions, and Health*. Boston: Shambhala

Publications, 1997. The discussions in this book, between His Holiness the Fourteenth Dalai Lama and a group of prominent physicians, psychologists, and meditation teachers, shed new light on the mind-body connection and on the cross-cultural notion that the mind can have a direct, healing effect on the body.

JUSTICE, BLAIR. *Who Gets Sick: How Beliefs, Moods, and Thoughts Affect* ✓ *Health.* Rev. ed. Houston, Tex.: Peak Press, 2000. A broad spectrum of findings drawn from leading-edge medical research on the power of the mind to enhance health and diminish disease.

TÜLKU THONDUP. *The Healing Power of Mind: Simple Meditation Exercises for Health, Well-Being, and Enlightenment.* Boston: Shambhala Publications, 1998. Harvard scholar and Tibetan Buddhist monk Tülku Thondup presents a lucid explanation of how meditation can, and should, become part of daily life and how the attainment and retention of a peaceful mind can ease stress and suffering. Includes many easy-to-use exercises that contribute to healing, relaxation, and the acceptance of present circumstances.

Mind and Medicine in Tibetan Buddhism

CLIFFORD, TERRY. *Tibetan Buddhist Medicine and Psychiatry: The Diamond Healing.* York Beach, Me.: Samuel Weiser, 1984. A comprehensive introduction to the esoteric Tibetan art of healing, written by an American psychiatric nurse who traveled to Tibet, Nepal, and Northern India to research traditional Tibetan medical methods of working with mental illness. An insightful and very clear description and explanation of many Tibetan Buddhist medical practices.

DALAI LAMA, et al. *Mindscience: An East-West Dialogue.* Boston: Wisdom Publications, 1993. After more than ten years of collaborative investigation, Tibetan Buddhist scholars and Harvard Medical School researchers share their findings and discuss mind-body concepts. Contributors include many leading authorities from the fields of medicine, psychiatry, psychology, psychobiology, neurobiology, and education.

DHONDEN, DR. YESHE. *Healing from the Source: The Science and Lore of Tibetan Medicine,* trans. B. Alan Wallace. Ithaca, N.Y.: Snow Lion Publications, 2000. The basics of holistic Tibetan medicine in an easy-to-understand and accessible format, written by the physician to the Dalai Lama.

HAYWARD, JEREMY W., and FRANCISCO J. VARELA, eds. *Gentle Bridges: Conversations with the Dalai Lama on the Sciences of Mind*. Boston: Shambhala Publications, 1992. Discussions that took place during a meeting between several prominent Western scientists and His Holiness the Dalai Lama. Demonstrates many of the ways that Tibetan Buddhism can contribute to modern research on the mind.

HOUSHMAND, ZARA, ROBERT B. LIVINGSTON, and B. ALLAN WALLACE, eds. *Consciousness at the Crossroads: Conversations with the Dalai Lama on Brain Science and Buddhism*. Ithaca, N.Y.: Snow Lion Publications, 1999. Dialogues from a series of meetings between the Dalai Lama and eminent Western neuroscientists and psychiatrists.

VARELA, FRANCISCO J., ed. *Sleeping, Dreaming, and Dying: An Exploration of Consciousness with the Dalai Lama*. Boston: Wisdom Publications, 1997. This book features teachings from the Dalai Lama about the "shadow zones" of consciousness: the mental states that arise when we sleep, when we dream, and when we die. Topics include lucid dreaming, near-death experiences, and the very structure of consciousness itself.

Tibetan Buddhist Perspectives on Death and Dying

BOKAR, RINPOCHE. *Death and the Art of Dying in Tibetan Buddhism*, trans. Christiane Buchet. San Francisco: ClearPoint Press, 1994. A very simple, practical, and easy-to-understand explanation of death and dying according to the Tibetan Buddhist tradition.

CHAGDUD TÜLKU RINPOCHE. *Life in Relation to Death*, 2d ed. Cottage Grove, Ore.: Padma Publishing, 2000. Describes the dying process and provides brief but profound instructions on preparing for death. This book is written with simplicity and clarity and can be helpful reading for elderly people or friends who are dealing with life-threatening illnesses. Includes additional practical information on preparing a durable power of attorney for health care, a living will for designation of life-support treatment, and a letter of instruction directing one's final arrangements.

DALAI LAMA. *The Joy of Living and Dying in Peace: Core Teachings of Tibetan Buddhism*, trans. Donald Lopez. San Francisco: HarperSanFrancisco, 1997. The Dalai Lama's wise and gentle voice infuses this presentation of Buddhist wisdom on death and dying and includes his own thoughts about the end of life and about how to live a compassionate and tolerant life.

LATI RINBOCHAY and JEFFREY HOPKINS, trans. & eds. *Death, Intermediate State and Rebirth in Tibetan Buddhism*. Ithaca, N.Y.: Snow Lion Publications, 1985. Detailed description of the Tibetan Buddhist view of how people die, the stages of death, and the subtle physiological processes that occur at death as well as during deep meditation.

MULLIN, GLENN H., trans. and ed.. *Living in the Face of Death: The Tibetan Tradition*. Ithaca, N.Y.: Snow Lion Publications, 1998. A compilation of nine short Tibetan texts that include inspirational accounts of the deaths of saints, methods for training the mind in the transference of consciousness at the time of death, and meditation techniques to prepare for death.

PADMASAMBHAVA. *Natural Liberation: Padmasambhava's Teachings on the Six Bardos*, trans. B. Alan Wallace. Boston: Wisdom Publications, 1997. In this work, the great ninth-century Indian master who established Buddhism in Tibet describes in detail six bardo processes and shows how to transform them into vehicles for enlightenment.

RANGDRÖL, TSELE NATSOK. *The Mirror of Mindfulness: The Cycle of the Four Bardos*, trans. Erik Pema Kunsang. Boston: Shambhala Publications, 1989. Written by one of the most learned and accomplished masters of seventeenth-century Tibet, this book is an inspiring and helpful presentation of Tibetan Buddhist teachings on the endless cycle of experience, the four bardos—life, death, after-death, and rebirth.

SOGYAL RINPOCHE. *The Tibetan Book of Living and Dying*, ed. Patrick Gaffney and Andrew Harvey. San Francisco: HarperSanFrancisco, 1994. This is an exceptionally inspiring and readable book that introduces the philosophy and practices of Tibetan Buddhism, focussing on the teachings surrounding death and dying. The book examines the remarkable possibilities for healing that can occur when people begin to view death as another chapter of life.

The Tibetan Book of the Dead

EVANS-WENTZ, W. Y., ed. *The Tibetan Book of the Dead: Or the After-Death Experiences on the Bardo Plane, according to Lama Kazi Dawa-Samdup's English Rendering.* London: Oxford University Press, 2000. This first and most famous English translation has served as the model for subsequent translations.

FREMANTLE, FRANCESCA, and CHÖGYAM TRUNGPA, trans. and commentary. *The Tibetan Book of the Dead: The Great Liberation Through Hearing in the Bardo.* Boston: Shambhala Publications, 1987. This translation emphasizes the practical advice that *The Tibetan Book of the Dead* offers to the living, and contains many useful lessons in human psychology.

LAUF, DETLEF I. *Secret Doctrines of the Tibetan Books of the Dead,* trans. Graham Parkes. Boston: Shambhala Publications, 1989. Although not a direct translation of *The Tibetan Book of the Dead,* this volume offers an in-depth study of the process described in it-a path that leads from death, through the after-death state, to transformation and rebirth. Illustrations and diagrams accompany a psychological commentary that illuminates much about the Tibetan Buddhist belief in the bardos.

PADMA SAMBHAVA. *The Tibetan Book of the Dead: Liberation Through Understanding in the Between,* trans. Robert A. F. Thurman. New York: Bantam Books, 1994. This translation preserves the form and spirit of the original but has been written with the Western reader in mind. It contains an introduction to Buddhism, the preliminaries of meditation, and a commentary about the scripture that makes it an accessible and readable translation.

General Tibetan Buddhism

GESHE RABTEN and NGAWANG DHARGYEY. *Advice from a Spiritual Friend.* 3d ed. Boston: Wisdom Publications, 1996. This book is not only enjoyable to read but also full of useful advice about the way we can transform our lives by responding to daily problems with patience and joy rather than intolerance and discontent.

GESHE WANGYAL. *The Door of Liberation: Essential Teachings of the Tibetan Buddhist Tradition.* Boston: Wisdom Publications, 1995. Geshe Wangyal was the first Tibetan Buddhist teacher to establish a monastery in America, and this book contains the seven fundamental Buddhist texts that he considered essential for Western students.

JAMGON KONGTRUL. *The Torch of Certainty,* trans. Judith Hanson. Boston: Shambhala Publications, 2000. Written by a versatile and prolific Tibetan scholar of the nineteenth century who has been called the "Tibetan Leonardo." Jamgon Kongtrul describes the fundamental practices of Vajrayana Buddhism and reveals much about the richness and profundity of the Tibetan Buddhist tradition.

KALU RINPOCHE. *The Dharma That Illuminates All Beings Impartially Like the Light of the Sun and the Moon,* trans. Janet Gyatso. Albany, N.Y.: State University of New York Press, 1986. Discourses that were presented in the United States by Kalu Rinpoche. Kalu's profoundly moving depth of realization gives the reader exquisite insights into these fundamental Tibetan Buddhist teachings.

MILAREPA. *The Hundred Thousand Songs of Milarepa: The Life-Story and Teaching of the Greatest Poet-Saint Ever to Appear in the History of Buddhism,* trans. Garma C. C. Chang. Boston: Shambhala Publications, 1999. Milarepa was a radical and loving person who overcame disastrous life circumstances and mastered his own anger and desire for revenge. The wisdom expressed in the songs of this eleventh-century poet and musician shows others how to transform their hearts.

PATRUL RINPOCHE. *The Heart Treasure of the Enlightened Ones: The Practice of View, Meditation, and Action : A Discourse Virtuous in the Beginning, Middle, and End,* trans. Padmakara Translation Group. Commentary by Dilgo Khyentse. Boston: Shambhala Publications, 1992. Teachings by Dilgo Khyentse on the root text written by Patrul Rinpoche in the nineteenth century. An inspirational and very practical guide to establishing a daily practice that is in accord with the traditions of Tibetan Buddhism.

———. *Kunzang lama'i shelung: The Words of My Perfect Teacher,* trans. Padmakara Translation Group. Eds. Kerry Brown and Sima Sharma. San Francisco: HarperSanFrancisco, 1994. A great nineteenth-

century teaching that introduces the fundamental spiritual practices common to all Tibetan Buddhist traditions. Stories, quota-
tions, and references to everyday life make this a readable and useful
guide to inner transformation.

POWERS, JOHN. *Introduction to Tibetan Buddhism*. Ithaca, N.Y.: Snow
Lion Publications, 1995. A thorough and comprehensive overview
of Tibetan Buddhism. Although this is a substantial volume (500
pages), it is packed with information that is presented in an engag-
ingly clear way. The use of Western methodology to present the history, lineages, doctrines, and practices of Tibetan Buddhism makes
the book very user-friendly.

General Buddhism

BANCROFT, ANNE. *The Pocket Buddha Reader*. Boston: Shambhala Publications, 2001. Selections from Buddhist scriptures that deal with
topics such as the search for truth, life and death, and living in communities.

Dhammapada: Translation of Dharma Verses with the Tibetan Text, trans.
Dharma Publishing Staff. Oakland, Calif.: Dharma Publishing,
1985. A strikingly clear presentation of the Buddha's teachings on
self, desire, and ignorance translated from Pali into Tibetan by the
controversial and brilliant twentieth-century scholar Gedün
Chöpel. This book includes the Tibetan text, side by side with the
English translation. A beautifully presented volume, one of the
most lovely I have ever seen.

FIELDS, RICK. *How the Swans Came to the Lake: A Narrative History of
Buddhism in America*, rev. and updated. Boston: Shambhala Publications, 1992. Written with attention-getting style and flow, this
fascinating account of how Buddhism spread from Asia throughout
America is both easy to read and difficult to put down.

KHEMA, AYYA. *Being Nobody, Going Nowhere: Meditations on the Buddhist Path*. Boston: Wisdom Publications, 1988. Written by a Western Buddhist nun of extraordinary accomplishment, this book gives
clear, practical instructions on meditation and offers techniques for
overcoming conditioned mental habits, ideas, beliefs, and thinking

patterns. Presents a beautifully written outline of the Buddhist path that can be understood and appreciated by everybody.

KORNFIELD, JACK, ed. *Teachings of the Buddha.*, rev. and updated. Boston: Shambhala Publications, 1995. Drawn from popular sources of Indian, Chinese, Japanese, and Tibetan literature, these writings offer advice and instruction on Buddhist practices such as meditation, cultivating calm awareness, and living with compassion. Includes selections on the role of women in early Buddhism.

SALZBERG, SHARON. *A Heart As Wide As the World: Stories on the Path of Lovingkindness.* Boston: Shambhala Publications, 1999. A series of helpful and comforting short essays—full of anecdotes and self-disclosure—that distill the author's more than twenty-five years of experiences teaching and practicing meditation. Of interest to readers on any spiritual path.

TSOMO, KARMA LEKSHE, ed. *Buddhism through American Women's Eyes.* Ithaca, N.Y.: Snow Lion Publications, 1995. A collection of articles written by American women, sharing their thoughts on Buddhist philosophy, its practical application in everyday life, and the challenges of practicing Buddhism in the Western world.

YESHE, LAMA, and LAMA ZOPA RINPOCHE. *Wisdom Energy: Basic Buddhist Teachings.* 25th anniversary ed. Boston: Wisdom Publications, 2000. A simple and compelling introduction to Buddhism based on talks given by these two great lamas on their first teaching tour of North America. This book gives the reader the feeling of being in direct contact with two great masters.

INDEX